Penguin  Readers

THE SPY WHO CAME IN FROM THE COLD

JOHN LE CARRÉ

LEVEL

6

ADAPTED BY FIONA MACKENZIE
ILLUSTRATED BY KEVIN HOPGOOD
SERIES EDITOR: SORREL PITTS

PENGUIN BOOKS

UK | USA | Canada | Ireland | Australia
India | New Zealand | South Africa

Penguin Books is part of the Penguin Random House group of companies
whose addresses can be found at global.penguinrandomhouse.com.
www.penguin.co.uk www.puffin.co.uk www.ladybird.co.uk

The Spy Who Came in from the Cold first published by Victor Gollancz Ltd, 1963
This Penguin Readers edition published by Penguin Books Ltd, 2019

002

Original text written by John le Carré
Text for Penguin Readers edition adapted by Fiona Mackenzie
Text copyright © le Carré Productions, 1963
Illustrated by Kevin Hopgood
Illustrations copyright © Penguin Books Ltd, 2019
Cover illustration by Matt Taylor
Cover illustration copyright © Penguin Books Ltd, 2014

The moral right of the original author has been asserted

Printed and bound in Great Britain by Clays Ltd, Elcograf S.p.A.

A CIP catalogue record for this book is available from the British Library

ISBN: 978-0-241-39795-4

All correspondence to
Penguin Books
Penguin Random House Children's Books
80 Strand, London WC2R 0RL

Contents

Note about the story

John le Carré is an English author who worked for the British secret service in Germany. He knew a lot about **spying***, but he does not write true stories. This story happens in Germany, in the 1960s. At the end of World War II, in 1945, the **Soviet** Union and some of the eastern countries were communist. Communists believed everyone should be equal and have an equal amount of money. The western countries including Britain and the USA were capitalist – they believed that everyone was different and they should earn different amounts of money for different jobs. For many years, there was a "cold war" between the two groups which was fought by **spies** not soldiers. There was an "**Iron Curtain**" between the West and the East.

Berlin was in the GDR (German Democratic Republic/East Germany), but it was an international city, with four parts (sectors). Britain, the USA and France controlled the three sectors in the west and East Germany controlled the sector in the east. In 1961, the East German government wanted to control people's movements more strictly and built a high wall between the sector in the east and the ones in the west. There were places, called "**checkpoints**", controlled by **guards** on both sides, where people could cross the wall. But many people were killed by East German guards while they were trying to escape from the GDR over the wall.

*Definitions of words in **bold** can be found in the glossary on pages 104–108.

Before-reading questions

1 Look at the cover of the book. Write a list of adjectives that come to your mind when you look at it.

2 What does the word "spy" mean? Use the definition on page 108 to help you. What famous spies do you know about?

3 Make brief notes on what you know about these places, events and times:
   a the end of World War II
   b the 1960s
   c Berlin
   d East Germany
   e the Soviet Union.

4 Read the back cover of the book. Make two guesses about things that will happen in the story.

5 The British secret service and the East German secret service are important in this story. Look up "service" in a dictionary. Then say what you think a "secret service" does.

6 Look at these illustrations from the story. Explain what you think will happen in the story.

CHAPTER ONE
Checkpoint

The American gave Alec Leamas another cup of coffee and said, "Why don't you go back home and sleep? We can phone you if he comes."

Leamas did not answer. He just stared through the window of the West German **checkpoint**. The street near the hut was empty.

"You can't wait forever, sir," said the American. "Maybe he'll come another time."

"He's coming," said Leamas. "It's nearly dark now."

Leamas stood next to a policeman who was watching the East German checkpoint through **binoculars**.

"He's waiting for the dark," Leamas said. "I know he is."

"But he's nine hours late," said the American.

Leamas became angry. "He's an **agent** – one of *my* agents," he said. "He doesn't have a timetable. He's in danger. He's frightened. Mundt knows that Karl is **spying** for us, and Mundt's chasing him. Karl knows he has one chance to escape – let him choose the best time."

"How did Mundt know about Karl?" asked the American.

"Shut up!" replied Leamas, and then he added more quietly, "I don't know."

A bell rang suddenly inside the hut. They waited silently. High above the checkpoint, huge lamps came on, shining their yellow light on everything. The policeman with the binoculars started to speak in German.

"The car has stopped at the first checkpoint," he said. "There is one person in it – a woman. The East German **guards** are taking her to the hut to look at her documents. The document check is completed. The car is going to the second checkpoint.

"The woman is going inside the hut. The guards are checking inside the car. The woman is coming out, and the barrier pole has been raised. She is driving the car over the bridge, past the final East German guard and into West Berlin."

Leamas went out of the hut into the icy winter night. The small crowd of people that was always near the checkpoint stood silently, lit by the huge lamps. The people changed, but the faces did not – they always looked helpless and confused.

The car had passed the hut and stopped further along the street. Leamas had recognized the woman. He walked over to the car and spoke through the window to her. "Where is he?"

"They came for him," she replied, "but he escaped – he took our bicycle. He has some money and some false documents. He said that he will come over tonight at this crossing point."

"Tonight?" said Leamas. "Are you sure?"

"Yes, he has to," she replied. "All the other agents have been caught by Mundt."

"All of them – Ländser, too – as well as Paul, Viereck and Salomon?"

"Yes."

"How do you know?" he asked.

"Karl told me," she replied. "He trusts me, and he tells me everything."

Leamas did not reply. He was angry with his agent for talking to this woman about his work for the British secret service. He had met her once with Karl, who had brought her to a bar in West Berlin. Leamas had been angry that Karl had brought her to a meeting with him. "Stupid man," thought Leamas. "Agents are all the same – you train them to lie, to trust nobody and to protect themselves. But they don't listen."

He pulled a key from his pocket and gave it to the woman. "You'll need somewhere to stay," he said. "Go to Albrecht-Dürer Strasse, number 28A. I'll phone you when he comes."

He went back to the silent hut. The American was not there. "He's gone home," said the policeman. Leamas told the policeman that they were waiting for a man on a bicycle, and then he went to the window and waited. In front of him was the road, and to either side there was the Wall. It was a dirty, ugly thing built from big blocks of rough concrete, with barbed wire on top and in front of it.

"Sir! Look!" the policeman suddenly whispered. "It's a man with a bicycle."

Leamas recognized the man who was pushing the bicycle. It was Karl. "He's done it," thought Leamas. "He's got through the first checkpoint. There's just the second one now." Karl calmly **leaned** his bicycle against the Customs hut and disappeared inside. At last, he reappeared, got on his bike and an East German policeman raised the red-and-white barrier pole. He was through, he was coming towards them. He had done it.

At that moment, Karl seemed to hear a sound and know that there was danger. He looked over his shoulder and began to move faster. An East German guard was on the bridge, watching Karl as he came towards him. Suddenly, the **searchlights** came on, shining on Karl. Then there was the sound of shouting and a **siren**. The East German guard dropped to his knees and lifted his gun. The first shot seemed to push Karl forwards, and the second shot seemed to pull him back. But he was still moving, still on the bicycle, passing the guard who was still shooting at him. Then he fell from the bike to the ground. Leamas hoped that Karl Riemeck was dead so that the East German secret service could not hurt him when they **interrogated** him.

CHAPTER TWO

The Circus

The plane took off, and Leamas looked out of the window as West Berlin disappeared beneath him. Mundt had won. Leamas was leaving Berlin without any agents in East Germany. There had not been any agents when he arrived in Germany, and he had **recruited** them all himself. Now he was leaving in the same way as he had started. And this was all because of Hans-Dieter Mundt, the **Head of Operations** in the East German secret service. Mundt's agents had killed all of the agents that Leamas had recruited. Leamas knew that he had failed, and it was the end of his **career**.

The air hostess brought Leamas a whisky. She thought he was an interesting-looking man, with his grey hair and brown eyes in a handsome, bony face. She thought he was around fifty, and this was about right. She thought he was single, which was half-true. Long ago there had been a wife. Somewhere there were teenage children who were given money by their father, paid from a bank in London. He looked like a man who could make trouble, a man who was not quite a gentleman.

The taxi stopped outside a grey **government** building in Cambridge Circus. Leamas nodded to the man on the reception desk at the Circus, the British Overseas Intelligence agency, and

11

went to the head of the agency's office. Control shook hands with Leamas. "You must be tired," he said. "Please sit down."

Leamas sat down opposite a small electric fire. Control was smaller than Leamas remembered, but he still wore his old black jacket.

Today it was cold, and Control was wearing a brown sweater under the jacket. Control behaved in the way that he always behaved – like a gentleman who knew he had to be polite. But Leamas knew Control was not really interested in him. Control took a packet of cigarettes from his desk and gave one to Leamas. Then he sat down opposite him. There was a **pause**, and then finally Leamas said, "Riemeck's dead."

"Yes, I know," replied Control. "I suppose it was that woman who **betrayed** him."

"**I suppose so**." Leamas did not know how Control knew about the woman.

"Mundt had him shot," Control added. "And how did you feel? When Riemeck was shot, I mean?"

Leamas **shrugged**. "I was **bloody** angry," he said.

Control looked at him through half-closed eyes. "Didn't you feel more than that? Weren't you upset?" he asked, thoughtfully.

"Yes, of course I was upset," said Leamas.

"Did you like Riemeck?" asked Control.

Leamas shrugged. "I suppose so," he said.

"How did you spend the night after he was shot?" asked Control. "What did you do?"

"Control," Leamas said, angrily, "why are you asking me these questions?"

Control continued to talk thoughtfully. "Riemeck was the last agent," he said. "There was the girl they shot outside a cinema, then the man in Dresden and some others who were arrested. Then Paul, Viereck, Salomon and Ländser. And finally, Riemeck. That is quite a lot of people. I wondered whether you'd had enough of your job."

"What do you mean . . . enough?" asked Leamas.

"I wondered whether you were tired . . . **burned out**?"

Leamas was silent. Then at last he said, "You must decide."

When Control spoke again, it was in the same thoughtful way. "In our jobs, we don't care about each other, do we? But we aren't like that really, are we? I mean . . . we can't be out in the cold all the time. We have to come in from the cold. Do you see what I mean?"

Leamas understood. He sat silently again. Then when he spoke at last, he said, "Control, tell me. What do you want me to do?"

"I want you to stay out in the cold a little longer," said Control. Leamas said nothing, so Control went on. "In our work, we do bad things so that ordinary people can sleep safely in their beds, don't we?"

Leamas nodded.

"And since the war, our **methods** have become quite similar to the methods of the **other side**," Control continued. "But of course, *we* use these methods for the right reasons. We have to be as **ruthless** as them, even though our government's reasons are better than theirs."

"What is he saying?" thought Leamas. "I wish he would say what he means."

"That is why," Control continued, "I think we ought to try to **get rid of** Mundt."

"Why?" asked Leamas. "We've got no one left in Germany to protect. You just said this yourself. Riemeck was the last one."

Control looked at his hands for a while without speaking. Finally, he said, "That isn't quite true. But I don't think I need to tell you about it."

Leamas shrugged.

"Tell me," said Control, "are you tired of spying? If you are, we'll need to get a different person to do this job. What I am thinking about is not an ordinary job – we need to stop Mundt's **colleagues** from trusting him. They have to believe that he is a traitor – that he is working for us, not them – so that they will get rid of him for us."

Leamas sat quietly, so Control went on. "What do you know about Mundt?"

Leamas knew quite a lot about Mundt. In his mind, he saw the photograph of the East German **spy** in the Circus's files. He saw an unfriendly face and white-blond hair. "He's forty-two," replied Leamas. "He was born in Leipzig. He has quickly become a very important person in the East German secret service, and there are now two really important men – Fiedler and Mundt. Mundt's own colleagues hate him because he is so ruthless, and they are afraid of him."

Control nodded and then added to what Leamas had said. "He's a killer. He was in this country two years ago, working for an East German company. We know that he killed two of his own agents. He nearly killed our agent George Smiley, too. Mundt isn't a real Communist. He is just fighting a war – the Cold War."

"Like us," said Leamas.

Control did not smile. "George Smiley knows all about what happened here," he continued. "He isn't working for us any more, but I think you should talk to him. Then, why don't you stay with me for the weekend?"

"Thanks, I'd like to," said Leamas.

"We can talk more about things then," said Control. "I think you might make a lot of money from the other side. You can keep all the money you make."

"Thanks," said Leamas.

"Of course, you must only do the job if you want to . . . if you're sure that you're not burned out," added Control.

"If you want to make trouble for Mundt, I'll do it," said Leamas.

"Do you really feel that?" Control asked. "You mustn't think you have to say that, you know. After all, we all get burned out in the end, in this job. We don't hate or love anyone or anything – but we don't want there to be any more pain."

Leamas did not answer, and Control went on. "Isn't that what you thought after they killed Karl Riemeck? You didn't feel hate for Mundt or love for Karl. You didn't feel anything. I was told that you walked all night through the streets of Berlin after they killed him. Is that right?"

"Yes," said Leamas, then added, "I'd like to get rid of Mundt."

Control nodded understandingly. "Good. That's useful," he said. "Now, if you meet any old friends in the Circus, please don't discuss this with them."

"All right," said Leamas.

"In fact," continued Control, "make them think that you're angry because we've behaved badly to you. You must begin to build a new life after today."

No one was surprised when Leamas did not go back to Berlin. He had failed there, and of course he was too old now to work with spies abroad. He was given an easy job in the Circus's office that made **payments** to people working abroad.

However, everyone was surprised at how quickly Leamas **went downhill**. He was angry about the way the Circus had behaved towards him and spoke **bitterly** about it. He became dishonest, borrowing money from colleagues and not paying it back. At first, colleagues were kind to him, understanding that he was having a bad time at the end of his career. But he was rude to them, and he did not **shave** and his clothes were dirty. So they stopped going near him. He did not seem to care. He ate alone in the dining room, and people said that he had started to drink too much.

Then he disappeared from the Circus. He did not say goodbye to anyone. Soon everyone heard a story that someone had stolen money from the office where Leamas had worked. It had happened just before Leamas disappeared. People discussed it. Was Leamas a thief? For a week or two they wondered what had happened to him and where he had gone to, but soon he was forgotten.

CHAPTER THREE
Liz

Leamas lived in a small, dirty flat on the top floor of an old building. There was a **grocer's shop** on the ground floor. The flat had old, brown furniture and a brown carpet with holes. Bare light bulbs hung from the ceilings.

He needed a job. Mr Pitt, who worked at the **Labour Exchange**, offered him one at the Bayswater Library, but Leamas did not want to work in a library, so he said no. Leamas thought he recognized Mr Pitt. He was certain that he had seen him at the Circus during the war, but the other man never mentioned it.

Leamas spent a week working in a horrible factory and a week trying to sell **encyclopaedias** that nobody wanted. After he lost these jobs, he drank more and more at a pub near his flat. Soon, people were used to seeing him there and in the shops and on the streets near where he lived. He was a grey, dirty man who did not shave. He never spoke to anyone. He was a man who had to look in all his pockets to find a bit of money. His neighbours felt sorry for him.

Finally, Leamas took the job in the Bayswater Library. "The work will be easy for an intelligent man like you," said Mr Pitt.

Bayswater Library was an old building with lots of high

bookcases in rows. On the morning Leamas arrived there, he found a young woman on a ladder near one of the bookcases.

"I'm the new person," he said. "My name's Leamas."

She climbed down and shook his hand. "I'm Elizabeth Gold. Call me Liz," the young woman said. "Have you done this kind of work before?"

"No," he said.

"Well, I'm checking all the books at the moment," Liz said.

Liz was tall and bony, with long legs. Her face was long, too, and she seemed to be both plain and beautiful at the same time. Leamas thought that she was twenty-two or twenty-three.

"You need to check that all the books are on the shelves," she said. "There are boxes of cards. When you've checked the number on the book, you tick it on the card. Why don't you look at the history books?"

She took him to a different bookcase, where a shoebox of cards lay on the floor. She left him there and went back to her work.

At 1 p.m., Leamas was hungry and asked Liz Gold what happened about lunch. "Oh," she replied, looking a bit **embarrassed**. "I bring sandwiches. There's no café near here. You can have some of mine if you like."

Leamas shook his head. "No, thanks. I've got some shopping to do."

When Leamas returned, he smelt of whisky. He went back to his bookcase and started checking books again. At 6 p.m., Liz locked the library, and they left.

It was bitterly cold outside.

"Have you got far to go?" asked Leamas.

"No," said Liz. "My flat's about twenty minutes' walk away. What about you?"

"It's not far," he said. "Good night."

About three weeks after Leamas began to work at the library, Liz invited him to supper. At 5 p.m., she **pretended** that she had suddenly had the idea. She had already realized that he would not come if she invited him to come the next day or next week. Leamas did not seem very happy about visiting her, but he came. After that, there were many meals at Liz's flat. He always came when she asked him, but he never spoke much.

Liz always **suspected** that there was something wrong with Leamas. "One day," she thought, "he is going to disappear, and I'm never going to see him again." She said to him one evening, "You must go when you want to go, Alec. I'll never follow you."

His brown eyes looked at her for a moment. Then he said, "I'll tell you when I'm going to go."

One evening, she said, "Alec, what do you believe in? Don't laugh – tell me." She waited, and at last he shrugged and said nothing.

"But you *must* believe in something," she said. "Something like God – I know you do. Sometimes you look like you've got something special to do."

She saw Leamas's smile and hated it. "Alec, don't smile," she said. "It's true."

He stopped smiling. "Sorry, Liz, but you're wrong," he said.

Liz knew he was getting angry, but she continued speaking.

"You don't like conversations like this because you hate something, don't you?" she said. "You're like a man who is going to do something awful."

The brown eyes looked at her, and when he spoke, his voice frightened her. "If I were you," he said, "I wouldn't ask questions." And then he smiled gently. Liz hadn't seen him smile like that before – he was being kind to her now. "What do you believe in?" he asked. "Are you religious?"

"No, of course not. I don't believe in God," she replied.

"Then what do you believe in?"

"I believe in . . . I'm . . . I'm a Communist," she said, quickly.

He started to laugh. "Oh, Liz, no! You're not a bloody Communist!"

"I am," she said, looking embarrassed. She was angry that he laughed, but she was also happy that he did not care very much.

That night they became lovers. He left at 5 a.m. She could not understand why he seemed **ashamed**. She was not ashamed.

Leamas walked down the empty street towards a park. It was foggy, so he did not see a man standing by the entrance to the park. By the time Leamas got to the entrance, the man had gone.

Then one day, about a week later, Leamas did not come into work, and Liz was worried. The next morning she arrived early at the library, and by the end of the morning she knew he would never come back to his job. She had promised never to follow him, but he had promised to tell her when he was going away. Should she go and find him?

At lunchtime, she went to Leamas's flat. She went up the dark stairs and knocked on the door. No one came. She turned the handle, and the door opened. Quietly, she went into the flat. It was bitterly cold and dark, but she could see a shape lying on the bed in the corner. She opened the curtains. Leamas was **sweating**, and his eyes were closed. He had not shaved for days, and Liz could see his dark beard against the white of his face. She was frightened, but she soon decided what to do. In the next few hours, she ran to the chemist to buy medicine, bought soup and soft biscuits, and made tea.

She held Leamas's head so he could drink and eat, whispering his name over and over again. At last, he stopped sweating and relaxed, and he fell asleep.

Then Liz cleaned the flat. When he woke, it was 8.30 p.m. "Alec, don't be **cross** with me. You're ill. You need me to look after you," she said.

For six days, she made him eat and helped him to wash and shave. Watching him get stronger after his illness, she thought she'd never been so happy. He did not speak much, and once, when she asked him if he loved her, he said he did not believe in happy endings to stories. She often lay on the bed with her head close to his.

Then, on Friday evening when she came home, he was dressed, but he had not shaved. She was afraid, although she did not know why. She cooked their supper while Leamas sat on the bed without speaking. While they were eating, she suddenly cried out, "Alec! Are you leaving?"

He took her hands in his and kissed her in a way he had never done before. He spoke quietly, but she did not understand what he said. She only knew that it was the end.

"Goodbye, Liz," he said. "Goodbye." And then, he added, "Don't follow me. Not again."

Liz nodded, and she went out into the bitter cold of the street outside.

The next morning, Leamas went to the grocer's shop downstairs and ordered **a number of** things. When the man had put them in a bag, Leamas picked it up. "I'll pay for these later," he said.

The grocer smiled politely and said, "I'm sorry, but you can't do that."

"Why not?" asked Leamas, angrily.

The other customers in the shop looked at each other nervously.

"I don't know you," replied the grocer.

"Don't be stupid. I've been coming in here for four months," said Leamas.

"You must pay for the **groceries**," said the grocer. "I don't know you, and I don't like you. Now get out of my shop." And he put out his hand to take the bag away from Leamas.

The other customers were not certain what happened next. Did the grocer push Leamas or not? They saw that Leamas hit the grocer with his left hand while he was still holding the bag in his right hand.

Some of the customers thought he hit the grocer twice, once on his neck with the side of his left hand and then with his left elbow. But he moved so quickly that they were not really certain what he did. They saw the grocer fall over and lie completely still on the floor.

There was **evidence** at his **trial** that Leamas had broken the bones in the grocer's **jaw** and in one of his cheeks. Leamas's lawyer did not disagree, and Leamas was **sentenced** to three months in prison. Some people learned about the trial in small **articles** in the newspapers.

CHAPTER FOUR

Ashe contacts Leamas

After three months, Leamas left the prison. It was a beautiful, sunny day, and there were bright flowers everywhere. He decided to walk across the parks in the centre of London and have a big meal at a café near Charing Cross Station. He was carrying a parcel with clothes and documents in it. He decided that he did not need the clothes, and he wanted to get rid of the parcel, but it was too big to put in a rubbish bin.

After a while he sat down on a wooden seat. Then he left the parcel on the seat and walked away.

Leamas heard a shout and looked back over his shoulder. There was a man holding the parcel in his hands. Leamas shrugged and walked on. There was another shout and Leamas heard someone running. A tall man with short brown hair stopped next to him.

"This is your parcel, isn't it?" he said. "Why didn't you stop when I called you?"

"You can put it back on the seat," said Leamas. "I don't want it."

"You can't just leave it there," said the man.

"I bloody well *can* leave it there," said Leamas. He was going to move on, but the stranger stood in front of him with the parcel.

"Why are you being so rude?" asked the stranger. "I was trying to be helpful."

"If you are just trying to be helpful, why have you been following me for the last half an hour?" asked Leamas.

Leamas saw that the man was thinking quickly about what to say next. "He's quite good at his job," he thought.

"I thought you were somebody I once knew in Berlin," the stranger replied.

"So you followed me for half an hour?" Leamas's brown eyes looked carefully at the man.

"It hasn't been half an hour. I saw you a few minutes ago, and I thought you were Alec Leamas. I borrowed some money from him. That's why I followed you. So if you *were* Alec, I could pay the money back."

Leamas thought then that maybe the man was not very good at his job. It was not a very good story. "I'm Leamas," he replied. "Who are you?"

The stranger told Leamas that his name was Bill Ashe. Ashe told Leamas a long story about how they had met in Berlin and why Ashe had borrowed money from Leamas.

"I was very embarrassed that I had to borrow money from you," said Ashe.

"Of course I remember you," said Leamas. "Of course."

Leamas and Ashe talked in the café for hours. A small man in glasses sat at the next table and read a very boring book.

At last, Ashe pulled his **chequebook** out of his pocket and started to write a cheque for twenty pounds. Leamas looked embarrassed and stopped him. "I haven't got a bank account at the moment," he said. "I've just returned from abroad. Could you let me have **cash**?"

"Of course," Ashe said. "Meet me here tomorrow at one o'clock, and I'll bring you cash."

When they left the café, Leamas left the parcel of clothes there. Ashe got in a taxi near the café, and Leamas waved till it disappeared. Leamas guessed that he was still being followed, so for several hours he walked and got on and off buses and trains. Finally, he walked to a house in West London. When he knocked on the door, Control opened it. "Come in," he said. "I've borrowed George Smiley's house."

"I was followed till lunchtime," Leamas said. Then he told Control the story of his life since he hit the grocer, ending with his meeting with Ashe that day.

"I'm sorry we couldn't help you while you were in prison," Control said. "And I heard that you were ill. I'm sorry about that, too. How long were you ill?"

"About ten days," replied Leamas.

"Oh dear," said Control. "You were ill for ten days with no one to look after you?"

There was a very long silence. Then Control said, "You know that the girl is a Communist, don't you?"

"Yes," said Leamas. There was another long silence. Then he said, "You mustn't **involve** her in this. I'll look after her myself when I return. I just want you to forget her."

"Of course we won't involve her," replied Control.

"Who was the man called Pitt in the Labour Exchange?" asked Leamas.

"I don't know anyone called Pitt," said Control.

"Oh, I'm sure you don't," said Leamas, crossly. Then he said, "Why isn't Smiley here?"

"Didn't he tell you when you visited him?" replied Control. "He doesn't like the job that you're going to do."

"No, we just talked about Mundt," said Leamas. "But does he agree that it has to be done?"

"Yes," replied Control. "He knows why we need to do it, but he is like a doctor who is tired of seeing blood. He is happy for other people to do the **operations**."

Then Leamas asked, "How do we know that I was contacted today by the right person? Are you certain that he works for the East Germans?"

Control replied calmly. "Don't worry, Leamas. We've organized things." Then he put his hand on Leamas's shoulder. "This is your last job," he said. "Then you can come in from the cold . . ."

Leamas nodded to Control and quietly left the house. He went out into the cold.

CHAPTER FIVE
Kiever

When he met Ashe the next day, Leamas smelt of whisky. But Ashe was very happy to see him and gave him an envelope of cash – twenty £1 notes. "Thanks," said Leamas, who had not shaved and was wearing a dirty shirt. He called the waiter and ordered drinks. When the drinks arrived, Leamas's hand shook as he poured some water into his whisky. Ashe talked a lot about himself while they had lunch. He told Leamas about a friend called Sam Kiever who paid him and other people to write articles about the United Kingdom for foreign newspapers. Leamas just let Ashe talk while he drank a lot. He did not talk about himself, and he did not ask any questions.

"You don't know Sam, do you?" asked Ashe at last.

"Who's Sam?" asked Leamas, looking confused.

Ashe sounded quite cross when he replied. "Sam. Sam Kiever. The man I was telling you about," he said. "Maybe you've met him."

"I don't think so."

There was a pause. "What do you do these days? What job, I mean?" asked Ashe.

Leamas shrugged. "Nothing much," he replied.

"What was it that you did in Berlin?" asked Ashe. "Weren't you one of those cold-war people?"

Leamas was surprised at the direct question. "Ashe must want to recruit me quickly," he thought.

"I was just doing things for the Americans," he answered, pretending to be angry. "That's what we all did."

"You know," said Ashe, "I've been thinking that you ought to meet Sam. You'd like him. Where do you live? Tell me, and then I can **get in touch** with you and bring Sam."

"I don't live anywhere," said Leamas. "I haven't got a job or any money. I just sleep where I can. The company that I worked for behaved badly to me."

Ashe looked upset. "You must come and stay with me," he said.

"I can't do that," replied Leamas. "I'll be all right. I'll get a job. I've had jobs before." And then he continued, still sounding angry. "I had jobs after they got rid of me. I worked in a horrible factory. I sold encyclopaedias. I got bored in a library."

"Leamas, you need a better job," replied Ashe. "You worked in Berlin for years, so you must speak German well. There are lots of things you could do. But you need to know useful people, don't you see?" Ashe sounded almost happy now. "Come and stay with me. Where are your things?"

"I haven't got any," said Leamas. "Everything I had was in the parcel, and I left that in this café."

Ashe lived in a small flat in Dolphin Square. There was not much furniture, and there were a few pictures from Germany. It was what Leamas had expected. Ashe made some tea, and then he said that he had to go out and do some shopping.

"Why don't you get some sleep, Alec?" he said to Leamas. "You look really tired." Then he touched Leamas gently on his shoulder and went out.

A few minutes later, Leamas went out, too, carefully leaving the door unlocked. He went to one of the public telephones on the ground floor and rang a number. "I'm ringing about Mr Sam Kiever," Leamas said to the voice that answered the phone. "He is coming to a meeting this evening at this address." Then he gave the voice the address in Dolphin Square. "I'll give the information to Control," said the voice.

Leamas was woken up by Ashe returning. With him was a small, fat man with grey hair who was wearing an expensive suit. He sounded like a foreigner. Perhaps he was German – Leamas was not sure. He said that his name was Sam Kiever.

They went to eat at a Chinese restaurant. The food was good and so was the wine, and Ashe paid the bill. Then they went to a bar, and Ashe continued to buy Leamas drinks – Leamas was drinking whisky now. Kiever seemed a bit bored. Then Leamas leaned across the table and said to Ashe, "Now tell me what is going on!"

"What do you mean, Alec?" Ashe sounded surprised.

"I mean that you followed me from prison yesterday," Leamas said, quietly. "You've told me a stupid story about meeting me in Berlin. You've given me money that you didn't owe me. You've bought me expensive meals, and now I'm staying at your flat. I'm asking why."

There was silence, and then Kiever spoke. "You go home," he said to Ashe. "I'll talk to Mr Leamas."

After Ashe had gone, Leamas leaned forward across the table again and said, "Are you going to tell me what's going on?"

Kiever nodded. "Of course. I told Ashe to contact you."

"Why?"

"I'm interested in you. I want to make a **suggestion** to you. I have a company that asks people to write interesting articles for my customers abroad. You've got memories of your international experience that one of my customers will pay for. They pay quickly, and then they ask for more information. They are happy to pay money into foreign banks."

Leamas said nothing. "Why is the other side hurrying?" he thought. Then he answered his own question in his head. "I'm a man with no money, who has just come out of prison, and I'm angry with the secret service that I worked for. A man like me would want to be paid by the other side for his **knowledge**."

"They'd have to pay me a lot for my knowledge," he said, quietly.

"My customer is offering a first payment of fifteen thousand pounds," said Kiever. "My customer wants to talk to you now, and you can have the money as soon as you have talked to him. You will receive another five thousand pounds if you give my customer more information during the next year. And you will get help to move to any country in the world."

"How soon do you want an answer?" asked Leamas.

"Now," said Kiever. "You will meet my customer tomorrow and talk to him. Then he will arrange for someone to write down your memories."

"Where would I meet your customer?" asked Leamas.

"It would be simpler to meet outside the United Kingdom," replied Kiever. "My customer has **suggested** a meeting in Holland."

"I haven't got a passport," said Leamas.

"I have a passport for you," said Kiever, calmly. "We're flying to The Hague tomorrow morning at nine forty-five. Shall we go to my flat?"

Kiever's flat was in an expensive part of London. He didn't want to talk, and Leamas realized that he was nervous. They were both nervous. Kiever took Leamas to a bedroom, and the next morning he was woken by Kiever at 6 a.m.

"I haven't got any **luggage**," said Leamas.

"I've organized your luggage and a British passport," replied Kiever. The passport had his name and **details** and a photograph. Leamas looked at the date on it.

"This passport **runs out** very soon," he said to Kiever.

"My customer doesn't want you to be able to go to other places easily," replied Kiever, laughing.

As Kiever answered, Leamas felt nervous again. His life would never be the same after today.

"You won't need any money," Kiever said. "The customer is paying for everything."

CHAPTER SIX
The house by the sea

After the plane landed in The Hague, Kiever and Leamas went quickly through the airport. "Have a nice stay in Holland," said the Dutch passport officer.

As they walked through the airport to the exit, Leamas looked back. He saw a man with glasses standing reading an English newspaper. He was small, and he looked worried.

Leamas and Kiever got into a car in the car park. The driver never spoke as she drove them out of The Hague. Leamas had been there during the war, and he guessed that they were travelling towards the coast. After a short time, the car stopped at a small house by the sea, and a friendly woman opened the door and let them in. Leamas saw a man in a raincoat getting out of another car.

"Welcome," the woman said. "Did you have a good journey?"

"Yes," replied Kiever. "It was a very good flight."

"That's good," she replied, and she disappeared. During Leamas's stay in the house, she brought meals to them, usually bread and cold meat.

Then Kiever opened the front door, and the man in the raincoat came in. He was the same height as Leamas but older. He shook Leamas's hand.

"My name is Peters," he said. "Did you have a good flight?"

"Yes" replied Kiever, quickly.

"Mr Leamas and I have a lot to discuss," said Peters to Kiever. "You can leave now."

Kiever smiled. "Goodbye and good luck," he said to Leamas and held out his hand.

Leamas nodded, but did not shake his hand. Kiever left the house quietly. Peters went into a room at the back of the house, and Leamas followed him.

"Listen," said Leamas, suddenly, sounding very nervous. "We both know why we're here. I'm a **defector**, and you're going to pay me for information. You don't all have to pretend that you like me and want to be nice to me."

"Kiever told me that you were a proud man," replied Peters, sitting down at a table. He spoke English very well. Leamas guessed that he was Russian, but he was not sure. He sat down, too.

"Kiever told you what we are going to pay you, didn't he?" asked Peters.

"He said that you would pay me fifteen thousand pounds now," replied Leamas. "And he said that you would pay me another five thousand pounds if I talk to you during the next year."

"Yes, that's right," replied Peters.

"I won't accept the five thousand pounds, and I won't talk to you during the next year," said Leamas. "You know that I can't do that. I want to take the fifteen thousand pounds and get away. If I tell you everything I know, I will have to disappear. The British secret service will know what I've done and look for me immediately."

Peters nodded, and then he said, "But you could come somewhere safer with us, couldn't you?"

"Are you asking me to come behind the **Iron Curtain**?" asked Leamas.

Peters nodded again.

"I don't want to do that," Leamas said, very quickly.

Peters nodded, then said, "Shall we start?"

During the morning of the first day, Peters asked questions about what Leamas had done during the war. Leamas told him about being in the army and then getting a number of different jobs because he spoke Dutch, German and French. Leamas had learned the languages when he lived in Holland because his father had an engineering factory there. The British secret service had trained him, and he had worked with spies in Holland and Norway during the war. After the war, he had gone to Berlin.

Peters saw that Leamas was sweating. He saw a man who wanted to betray his country but was upset and uncomfortable. This was what Leamas wanted him to see.

Leamas watched Peters, too, and decided that he was good at his job. Peters listened carefully, only asking a few questions. Leamas told Peters about starting to work in Berlin in the 1950s. The British needed to get information from East Germany, but it was hard to find good agents. At last, in 1959, Karl Riemeck made contact with him, first by leaving photographs and documents in Leamas's car. Then they had met. Riemeck worked for the **Praesidium** of the East German government. He did not have a very important job, but he gave Leamas enormous amounts of useful information about Praesidium meetings. He also gave Leamas the names and jobs of people in the East German secret service.

"Did Riemeck give you all the information you're telling me about?" Peters asked.

"Yes, of course," replied Leamas.

"I see," said Peters. "Please go on."

Peters filled Leamas's glass with more whisky, as he had done often during the **interrogation**, and Leamas continued. Bit by bit, he told Peters all about Riemeck's work. He gave the names of other agents who Riemeck had introduced to Leamas and the dates they had started being agents. He explained what the Circus had thought and how much they had paid Riemeck. Peters was pleased at how good Leamas's memory was even though he was drinking so much.

"I don't believe you," said Peters after a while. "Riemeck's job wasn't important enough. He couldn't do all this on his own."

"He did do it," said Leamas, suddenly becoming angry.

"Didn't the Circus wonder whether there was another person helping him?" asked Peters.

"No," replied Leamas.

"Oh, that's interesting," said Peters, thoughtfully. Then, after a moment, he said, "You heard about Riemeck's woman, didn't you?"

"What about her?" asked Leamas.

"She was murdered a week ago. She was shot as she left a flat in West Berlin."

Leamas was very surprised. "She was in West Berlin – why wasn't she safe there?" he thought. "Did Riemeck tell her the name of another East German agent? And did that agent arrange for someone to kill her so she didn't tell anyone the name?"

That night, Leamas continued to think about the woman's death. "Why didn't Control tell me about it?" he wondered. He remembered his question to Control about why they should get rid of Mundt, and Control's answer. He had asked: *"Why? We've got no one left in Germany to protect. You just said so yourself. Riemeck was the last one."* And Control had replied: *"That isn't quite true. But I don't think I need to tell you about it."* "What did Control know that he didn't tell me?" Leamas thought. "And *why* didn't he tell me?"

That night he thought about the murdered woman, and then he thought about Liz.

CHAPTER SEVEN
Bad news

Peters arrived at the house at 8 a.m. the next morning and immediately started the interrogation again. He asked Leamas about his time in London since leaving Berlin. Leamas told him the story that he had agreed with Control. He told him about working in the office at the Circus that made payments to people working abroad. He explained that he was bored, that he had started to drink and that he had been asked to leave. Peters was interested in his last job at the Circus.

"Tell me what you did," he said.

"I made payments to agents," replied Leamas. "I got letters telling me to write cheques, but I never had the names of the agents or where they were in the world. But sometimes they gave me too much information, so I did know who was going to be paid. I made a list last night of all the payments that I could remember."

Leamas gave Peters his list, and Peters read it carefully. "This is good," he said. "Very good."

Leamas continued. "I remember an operation called Rolling Stone best," he said. "I made two trips abroad because I was working on it. One trip was to Denmark – to Copenhagen – and one was to Finland – to Helsinki. I had to **deposit** money in banks."

"How much money?"

"Ten thousand dollars in Copenhagen and forty thousand dollars in Helsinki," replied Leamas.

"Who was the money for?" asked Peters.

"I don't know," replied Leamas. "Control didn't tell me."

"Was Control managing the operation himself?" asked Peters.

"Yes," said Leamas. "I had some information but not all of it."

He gave a lot more information about Rolling Stone to Peters. He explained that the Circus gave him false documents for the person who would get the money from the Danish and Finnish banks. He told Peters that some payments were made before he was working in the office. Peters wrote everything down carefully.

"What were the names the person had to use to **withdraw** the money from the banks?" he asked.

"Horst Karlsdorf and Adolf Fechtmann," said Leamas.

"Those are both German names," said Peters.

"Yes, but the person wasn't German," replied Leamas, quickly.

"Why are you sure about that?" asked Peters.

"Because I was Head of Operations in Berlin. I would have known if we were paying large amounts of money to an East German agent," said Leamas, beginning to sound angry.

"Are you sure there wasn't another agent for the British working in East Germany?" asked Peters.

"I'm sure there wasn't!" shouted Leamas, now very angry. He remembered what Control had said. *"Give them your information,* *and let them **work out** what to think. It will be good to make them think that they know more than you."*

Peters nodded as if he understood something about Leamas. He thought that Leamas was angry that the Circus might have an agent in East Germany who Leamas did not know about. "You are a very proud man, Mr Leamas," he said.

Peters left the house at lunchtime on the second day. He did not appear that afternoon, and he did not appear the next morning, either. Leamas asked the woman who brought his meals where Peters was, but she just smiled and shrugged. At last, he decided to go for a walk by the sea. There was a girl on the beach throwing pieces of bread to the seabirds. Leamas thought about Liz. He wanted to do simple things with her, like throw bread to seabirds. He wanted love and to have a new life with her. He would be home soon – perhaps in two weeks. He would have plenty of money, and he could come in from the cold.

When he got back to the house, he heard the woman make a phone call. Finally, at 3 p.m., Peters arrived, and, as soon as Leamas saw him, he knew that there was a problem. Peters did not take off his coat and did not sit down.

"I've got bad news for you," said Peters. "I heard it this morning. The police are searching for you in England. They're checking ships and planes that are leaving the country."

"Why do they want me?" thought Leamas. He was shocked and confused, but he stayed silent.

"There are articles in all the newspapers, but they just say that police want to talk to you. They don't say that you have **defected**, but they mention the **Official Secrets Act**, so people will think that you are a spy."

"This wasn't part of the plan. I'm supposed to be able to go home in two weeks," he thought. "Why has Control done this?" Leamas felt angry with Control, and worried, but he tried to think quickly. "What am I going to do?" he asked himself. "I could refuse to talk any more to Peters. But if I stop acting my part now, the operation against Mundt will fail."

"Every police force in Western Europe will be looking for you," said Peters. "You've got a choice. You can let us look after you – we can arrange to take you to the East. Or you can go away alone – but you will definitely be caught. You don't have any money, your passport runs out in ten days and you don't have any false documents."

"If I come with you, what will you do with me when you have completed your interrogation?" asked Leamas.

Peters shrugged. "We'll give you a new passport, probably. Then you can go where you want."

Leamas stared out of the window. At last, he said, "All right, I'll come."

"There's no plane to the East until tomorrow," said Peters. "But there's a flight to Berlin in an hour. We need to leave now."

At the airport, Leamas bought a newspaper. He found an article about himself, and he wondered whether Liz had seen it.

CHAPTER EIGHT
Alec's friend

Liz was very sad after Alec disappeared. Of course, she heard about him hitting the grocer and going to prison. The members of her Communist Party **Branch** talked about it at a meeting, though they did not know about her and Alec. "He knew he was going to do it," she thought. "He knew it when he said goodbye to me. But why?"

Once, she went to his flat and talked to his **landlord**. She did not know why she did it, but the landlord spoke kindly about Alec, so she was pleased she had gone. He told her that a friend of Mr Leamas, a small, shy man with glasses, had come to see him. The friend said that Mr Leamas had asked him to pay all his rent. Mr Leamas was a strange man, the landlord said, but it was very good of him to send his friend to do that.

She continued to work at the library and thought about Alec all the time. Then a man came to see her at her flat. He was a short man who wore glasses and an expensive suit. She thought he must be Alec's friend. The man said that he came from the police, from **Special Branch**. Then he asked her about Alec.

"I believe you were friendly with Alec Leamas," he said, worriedly. He looked kind, and Liz trusted him without knowing why. So she answered him honestly.

"Yes," she said. "How did you know?"

"Oh, we found out by chance," he replied. "When you go to prison, you have to give the names of your family, or the people closest to you. Then they can be informed if anything happens to you. And Alec gave your name."

"I see." Liz was surprised and confused.

"Did anyone know that you were friendly with Alec?" the small man went on.

"No."

"Did you go to the trial after he hit the grocer?"

"No."

"Did any people from the newspapers call you?" he asked.

"No, I've told you," said Liz. "No one knew. Not even my parents."

The small man thought for a moment, then asked, "Were you surprised when Alec hit the grocer?"

Liz wondered if she was talking too much to him, but she wanted to talk to someone about it. It did not matter now. "Yes, I was surprised," she said. "But I think he knew that he was going to do it."

"What do you mean?" the man asked, quickly.

"Well, the night before he did it, we had supper together," she replied. "It was a special meal, and I asked him, 'Is this goodbye?'"

"What did he say?" said the small man.

"He said that he had something that he must do. I didn't really understand," Liz said.

There was a very long silence, and the small man looked more worried than ever. Liz suddenly felt **terrified** for Alec, and she did not know why.

"Why do you think he asked people to inform you if anything happened to him?" the man asked.

Liz felt her face turn red. "I was in love with him," she replied. "Please don't ask any more questions. Please go now."

The small man got up to go, then took out a card from his pocket and put it gently on the table.

"If you ever want any help or if anything happens about Alec, ring me," he said. "Do you understand?"

"Who are you?" asked Liz.

"I'm Alec's friend," he replied. "Oh . . . just one more question. Did Alec know that you are a member of the Communist Party?"

"Yes, I told him," she replied.

"Does the Party know about you and Alec?" he asked.

"No, I told you!" she shouted. "No one knew." Then suddenly she cried out, "Where is he? Tell me where he is! I can help him. I can look after him."

"He's abroad," replied the small man, quietly. "I'm sorry that he told you that he had something special to do."

"Who are you?" she asked again.

"I'm Alec's friend," he repeated. "Don't worry. We'll look after you – with money and that kind of thing."

He went out of the door, and she heard a car start in the street. Then she remembered the card and picked it up off the table. There was only a name, address and telephone number on it. There was nothing to say what his job was: 'Mr George Smiley, 9 Bywater Street, Chelsea'. It was very strange.

CHAPTER NINE

To the East

Leamas sat on the plane to West Berlin and wondered again why things had changed. Why had his **defection** been discovered so soon? Control knew, because Control had done this, but Leamas did not know. He also remembered Control's advice when he had stayed at his house for the weekend. *"Get angry. Drink a lot. Confuse them by telling them that something is true one day, then telling them that the same thing is not true the next day. Make them work hard to get your information. Make them believe they have worked out that Mundt has betrayed their side to us. They already have information that we gave them before you became involved. You are taking them the last parts of the story."*

After the plane landed, Peters led Leamas quickly through the airport to a big black car, which was waiting in a car park. After they got into it, a smaller car pulled out of the same car park in front of them. Both cars moved quickly through the streets of Berlin, and Leamas was surprised at how easily they crossed out of the West and into the East. Leamas thought that they would stop in East Berlin, but the car kept moving.

"Where are we going?" he asked Peters.

"We're here," replied Peters. "We are in the German Democratic Republic."

"I thought we would go further east, to Russia," said Leamas.

"The East Germans want to talk to you," said Peters.

Leamas nodded his head, and Peters continued.

"I sent your information to them, and they are interested in it. They've never talked to anyone with your knowledge before."

"Who will interrogate me?" asked Leamas. "I know the names of most of the people in the East German secret service."

"Who do you think that you will meet?" replied Peters.

"Fiedler, who works for Mundt," said Leamas.

Leamas thought back to what he had learned about Fiedler. Leamas remembered that Fiedler had lived in Canada during the war, so he spoke good English. The photographs had shown a thin young man with dark hair and intelligent brown eyes. He was a man who worked alone and whose colleagues did not like or trust him.

He remembered what Control had said. *"Fiedler hates Mundt, and he is as clever as Mundt. He'd like to get rid of Mundt, so he is the person who is most useful to us. You will make him believe that Mundt is a **double agent**, working for us. But you mustn't make it obvious."*

Finally, the car arrived at a **farmhouse** and stopped outside it. By now, it was night, and in the light of the moon Leamas saw two men get out of the small car, which had also stopped. He could also see a thin man sitting in the back of it. Peters took Leamas into the old farmhouse, which smelled like a place where nobody lived.

He and Leamas sat down in a room with old, dark-coloured furniture, and photos of **Soviet** leaders on the walls.

After a few silent minutes, the door opened and a short, thin man came in, carrying a bottle of whisky and two glasses. He was wearing a dark-blue suit that looked too big for him.

"Hello," he said to Leamas. "I'm Fiedler. I'm glad to see you. You've reached the end of your journey."

"What do you mean?" asked Leamas, quickly.

"I mean that you're not going any further east. Sorry."

Leamas remembered something Control had said. *"Make them dislike you, and then they will believe what you tell them more."* So he pretended to be very angry.

Leamas turned to Peters. "Is this true?" he shouted, angrily. "Tell me!"

Peters nodded. "Yes. We – the Soviet secret service – agreed to help our friends in the East German secret service and bring you here."

Leamas shouted at Fiedler, "You knew I wouldn't defect to a little, unimportant place like the GDR. That's why you sent a Russian!"

"We had help from the Russians to take you to Holland," said Fiedler. "In fact, we didn't want to bring you to East Germany. But we didn't know that your colleagues in Britain would find out about your defection so quickly. We had to do it because there are still things that you haven't told us."

Then Fiedler said something in Russian to Peters, who nodded and stood up. "Goodbye," Peters said to Leamas.

Leamas did not answer.

CHAPTER TEN
Details

That night, Leamas slept in a small, bare room with only a bed and a desk in it. To get to his room, he had to walk through another room with two beds in it. Later, he realized that the two men who slept there were guards. In fact, these guards were never far away from him while he was in the farmhouse.

The next morning, one of the guards brought some bread and bad coffee for breakfast. Leamas looked out of the window while he was having breakfast. The farmhouse was on the top of a high hill, and, below it, Leamas could see hills covered with tall trees. There were no houses, and a long way below in a valley he could see the road. There was no sound.

Fiedler came into the room. "Good morning," he said with a smile. "Finish your breakfast, and then we will talk."

"I've told Peters everything that I know," replied Leamas.

"Oh no you haven't," replied Fiedler. "You've only given us one piece of information that we didn't know. I'm talking about Rolling Stone, of course. And I'm sure that you can tell us more."

He took Leamas outside, and they went for a walk down the road into the valley and then along a path through the forest. Fiedler asked lots of questions. He asked about the building in Cambridge Circus in London and about the people who worked there. He asked about their families and where they lived.

Most of all, he wanted to know about why they worked for the Circus. "What do they believe in? What is their philosophy?" he asked.

"I don't know," said Leamas. "They don't believe in anything. They're just people."

"What makes them do these jobs, then?" asked Fiedler. He sounded confused.

"I don't know," said Leamas. Then he added, "I suppose they don't like Communists."

"I see," said Fiedler. "We kill people because we believe in something. It must be harder to kill people if you don't have a philosophy that you believe in."

"I don't know," replied Leamas. "And I don't care." He suddenly sounded tired.

They stopped while Fiedler gave Leamas a cigarette and lit it for him. About an hour after they had left the farmhouse, they reached the top of a hill. Looking back, Leamas could see the farmhouse across the valley. He was enjoying the walk.

"We'll sit down for a moment," said Fiedler, "and then we must go back. Tell me more about Rolling Stone. Large amounts of money were deposited in banks in Copenhagen and Helsinki. What did you think they were for?"

"I told Peters," replied Leamas. "They were payments to an agent, probably behind the Iron Curtain."

"Why did you think so?"

"Well, they were very big payments, and it was very difficult to make them," replied Leamas. "And, of course, Control was involved, too."

"What do you think that the agent did with the money?" asked Fiedler.

"I don't know," said Leamas. "I don't even know if the money was collected. I just went to Denmark and Finland and deposited the money in the banks, and then I came back."

"What names did you use, and when did you go to each country?" asked Fiedler.

"In Copenhagen, I was Robert Lang. And in Helsinki, I was Stephen Bennett."

"And when did you go to each country?" asked Fiedler.

"I went to Denmark on 15th June of this year and to Finland on 24th September," replied Leamas.

"Did the banks ever write to you?"

"I don't know. If they did, the letters went to Control, I suppose," replied Leamas.

"You didn't know much," said Fiedler, "so it is possible that the Rolling Stone payments were to a double agent in the GDR."

"No," said Leamas. "I told Peters. That's impossible. I was **in charge**, and I knew about all the agents in East Berlin."

Fiedler did not reply. Instead, he went on. "You could help us to find out whether anyone withdrew any of the money from those banks. You could write a letter to each of the banks and ask for a **current statement**. We could send the letters from an address in Switzerland."

"How would that help you?" asked Leamas.

"If the money was withdrawn, we will know the date when the agent was there. That might be useful," said Fiedler.

"You're dreaming, Fiedler," replied Leamas. "You'll never find the person who the payments were for. You don't even know if he's an East German."

Fiedler looked out over the valley for a few moments before he spoke again. "We know that Rolling Stone was an operation against us," he said.

Leamas realized that Control's plan was working. Fiedler believed in Rolling Stone. "All right," he said. "I'll send the letters."

CHAPTER ELEVEN

Two letters

Leamas was still in bed the next morning when Fiedler brought the letters for him to sign. They each came from a different hotel in Switzerland. Leamas read the first letter:

To the Manager
Royal Scandinavian Bank
Copenhagen

    Dear Sir,
    I have been travelling for a few weeks and have not received any post from England. For this reason, I have not received your reply to my letter of 3rd March asking for a current statement of my joint account with Herr Karlsdorf. I don't want any more delay, so please could you send a statement to me at this address:
13 Avenue des Colombes
Paris XII, France.
I am sorry for this confusion.
Yours faithfully,
Robert Lang

"I didn't send them a letter on 3rd March," Leamas said.
"No, you didn't," replied Fiedler. "But if the bank thinks that

you did, they will be worried and will reply quickly."

The second letter was the same as the first one except for the names. Leamas signed the names on both letters. Fiedler thanked him and told him that someone would post the letters in Switzerland the next day. He expected to hear from his colleagues in Paris about the replies in about a week. "So we can go for walks and drive around the hills," said Fiedler. "And you can tell me more details about the Circus."

There were many more walks that week. Both men were relaxed, and Leamas talked a lot about his job and the Circus.

In the evenings, they ate together and talked in front of a fire. The two men began to like each other and almost to trust each other, although Fiedler did not understand why Leamas had wanted to defect.

Fiedler told Leamas that he had only been to England once, when he was a child. "But," Fiedler said, "Mundt worked there. Did you know that he worked in London?"

"Oh, yes," replied Leamas. "He killed two people while he was there. And he nearly killed my colleague, George Smiley, too."

"It was amazing that Mundt managed to escape, wasn't it?" said Fiedler.

"I heard that they didn't really want to catch him," replied Leamas.

"What?" said Fiedler.

"Someone told me that one of our people made some big mistakes," replied Leamas. "It was better to let Mundt escape than to let too many people find out about them."

"Did anyone suggest that there was another reason why the Circus let Mundt escape?"

"What do you mean?" asked Leamas.

Fiedler did not reply then, but as the days passed he started to seem **tense** and worried. One day, when they were driving in the hills, Fiedler made a long phone call from a phone box. Leamas wondered why he did not use a phone in the farmhouse.

Later, Fiedler said, "We must be careful. Both of us."

"Why? What do you know?" asked Leamas, quickly.

"You might have to look after yourself for a while," Fiedler said. "But don't worry. Everything will be all right."

He held Leamas's arm tightly and continued speaking. "Mundt has never done an interrogation before. I've always done them. Mundt likes to kill people, not talk to them, and I've often wondered why." His hand held Leamas's arm more tightly. "I've thought about it, Leamas. I think he killed British agents who might know too much about him. I think Mundt is a double agent, working for the Circus."

"You're crazy," said Leamas, angrily. "It's not true. I was in charge in Berlin. The Circus couldn't have an agent who I didn't know about – not an agent who was the Head of Operations for the East German secret service."

"That phone call," said Fiedler, "was about the reply to your letter to the bank in Copenhagen. Someone withdrew all the money from the account a week after you deposited it. It happened when Mundt was on a visit to Copenhagen."

———

In London, Liz had received a letter, too. It came from the organizers of the Communist Party in Britain.

Dear **Comrade**,

We have had an invitation from the Party in the German Democratic Republic for some of our members to visit Party Branches there. There are going to be visits for members of the Bayswater Branch to the Neuenhagen Branch in Leipzig. We asked for names of people who might be interested, and your name was given to us. We are sure that you are the right Comrade for this job. All costs will be paid by the Party in the GDR.

We are sure that you will want to accept this invitation. The visit will happen at the end of this month. Members will travel alone because the visits will happen at different times. Please let us know as soon as possible whether you can accept, and we will let you have more information.

Liz wondered who had given her name to the organizers. Then she remembered a man who she had met at a big meeting for all the London Branches. He had asked lots of questions. "Ashe, that was his name," she thought. "Perhaps it was him."

She felt excited because it was a trip abroad. After writing to accept the invitation, she saw Smiley's card. She remembered him saying, "Did the Party know about you and Alec?", and she smiled. The trip abroad would help her to forget about Alec.

CHAPTER TWELVE
Arrest

After their conversation in the car, Fiedler and Leamas drove back to the farmhouse in the dark. Fiedler parked the car at the side of the house, and as they walked towards it they saw three men standing near the front door.

"Fiedler, we want to talk to you. We're from Berlin," shouted one of them.

"What's going on?" said Fiedler. "Why aren't the lights on in the house?"

Fiedler walked towards the men. Leamas could not see the guards who usually stayed near him when he was at the house. He waited for a moment, then went inside. He could not switch the lights on because they were controlled from a central point by an unseen hand. Slowly and carefully, he walked in the darkness towards his bedroom. He walked into the guards' bedroom and realized that they were not there either, and then suddenly the door behind him closed. The room was completely dark. He smelled cigarette smoke from his own bedroom. Then he heard the key turn in the lock of the door behind him, and he knew that he could not escape.

Leamas remembered his training. He walked towards a chair that he knew was in a corner of the room and kicked it into the centre of the room. The people in the room knew that he was there, so he did not need to be quiet.

Counting his footsteps, he moved back from the chair and stood in one corner. He knew where the chair was, but they did not.

"Why don't you come in then?" he said in German. "I'm here in the corner. Come and get me."

There was no sound from the other room. "Come on then!" shouted Leamas. "Are you scared?"

At last, he heard one person moving forwards out of his bedroom, then another one. He heard the first one walk into the chair and cry out in pain. This was what he was waiting for. He moved forward, holding his left arm out in front of him until he touched an arm. He hit it gently, twice, and a voice very close to him whispered, "Hans, is that you?"

"Be quiet," whispered Leamas. At the same time, he reached out, got hold of the man's hair and pulled his head forward. He hit him hard on the back of his neck, then pulled him up again and hit the front of his neck. The man fell heavily to the floor and did not move. Then suddenly the lights came on, and the door behind Leamas opened, making Leamas turn round quickly. Something hit him on the back of his head, and he fell to the floor.

When Leamas woke, he was cold, and he could feel blood on his face. He was lying on a stone floor, and, when he tried to move, terrible pain went through his body. His hands and feet were held together behind his back by a chain. Above him, there was a bright light, and he was in a white, empty room.

He lay on the floor in pain for hours. At last, the door opened and Mundt came in, followed by two guards. Leamas looked at Mundt and remembered George Smiley telling him about Mundt's frightening eyes.

The two guards untied his arms and legs. He tried to stand, but they kicked him, so he fell down again. Then they pulled him along a corridor to a small room with a desk and two armchairs. Mundt sat at the desk, and the guards put Leamas in an armchair where he sat with his eyes closed.

"Give me a drink," whispered Leamas.

Mundt gave him a glass of water from a bottle on his desk. "Bring him something to eat," he said to the guards. They quickly brought a cup of soup and some pieces of sausage. Leamas ate and drank while they watched in silence.

"Where's Fiedler?" asked Leamas, finally.

"He's been arrested," replied Mundt.

"What for?" asked Leamas.

"He's working for the enemies of the GDR," Mundt said.

"I see," said Leamas. "You think Fiedler is working for the British secret service, and that I'm here to help him. You think I'm here to make the East German secret service believe you are an agent for the British. So you've arrested us both."

"That's right. You'll both **be put on trial**," replied Mundt. "*You* will also be put on trial for murder."

"So the guard died, did he?" Leamas replied.

Mundt nodded, and then he went on. "You aren't really a defector, of course. As soon as I read Peters's report, I knew why you were here. I knew that Fiedler would believe that I was a double agent because he hates me and wants my job."

"So you've won," said Leamas.

"Yes," replied Mundt. "Fiedler sent a report to the Praesidium yesterday that he didn't send to me. But I saw it, and I knew that he wanted to arrest me."

The pain all over Leamas's body was increasing. Suddenly there was shouting, and the door opened violently. Leamas could not open his eyes because of his pain, but he could feel that the room was full of people. He did not know what was happening.

Suddenly, there was silence, and then someone picked him up gently and carried him out of the room.

When he woke again, he was in a hospital bed, and standing beside it was Fiedler.

CHAPTER THIRTEEN

Branch Meeting

Leamas looked around the quiet hospital room and then at Fiedler, who was calmly smoking a cigarette.

"How do you feel?" asked Fiedler.

"Awful," replied Leamas. "They **beat me up**, you know."

"Yes," said Fiedler. "And you killed a guard."

"I guessed that I had," said Leamas, "but I had to protect myself. What happened to you?"

"Oh, Mundt's men beat me up, too," replied Fiedler. "And he interrogated me as well, but I knew that he would lose."

"Why?" asked Leamas.

"I had collected evidence against him," he replied. "Then you brought me the last piece of evidence that I needed – about the payments. I put it all in my report to the Praesidium. So while he and his men were beating us up, the members of the Praesidium were setting up a Tribunal."

"What's that?" asked Leamas.

"It's a secret trial," said Fiedler. "It will happen tomorrow. Mundt has been arrested, and you will give evidence against him."

Then a nurse brought Leamas some food, which he ate, although he still felt awful. Fiedler watched him without speaking.

"What will happen in the Tribunal?" asked Leamas.

"There are three judges. One of them – the President – is

in charge of the others," Fiedler said. "I will **put the case** against Mundt, and a clever man called Karden will defend him."

"Why can't Mundt defend himself?" Leamas asked.

"Mundt has asked for Karden to do it. I have been told that Karden will call a **witness**."

They sat in silence again, and then Fiedler spoke. "You must get some sleep," he said. "Tomorrow, you can talk."

Leamas went to sleep feeling pleased. He was pleased that Fiedler was on his side against Mundt, even though Fiedler was really on the other side – against the British secret service. And tomorrow, Mundt would receive a **sentence** of death.

———

At the same time, Liz was in Leipzig, where she had been for a few days. She was staying with a kind woman called Comrade Ebert, who was the secretary of the Communist Party's Neuenhagen Branch. Liz knew some German, so she could talk a little to people. She helped with work, giving books to people about the Party and visiting members who had not been to meetings recently. The Branch Meeting was on the fourth evening of her visit. There was going to be a discussion about "Working and living together after two wars", and Comrade Ebert told Liz that a lot of people would come. It was hard to make people come to the Branch Meetings in London, so Liz wanted to get ideas to take home. She was pleased that the meeting room was better than the one in London. But then only seven people came, and Liz was very upset.

Liz was waiting for Comrade Ebert to put on her coat after the end of the meeting, when a man opened the door.

"Comrade Ebert?" he asked.

"Yes," Comrade Ebert replied.

"I'm looking for an English comrade," he continued. "She is staying with you – Comrade Gold."

"I'm Elizabeth Gold," said Liz.

"My name is Holten. I'm from the Party," he said. He showed some papers to Comrade Ebert, who looked at them and nodded. Then she looked at Liz a bit nervously.

"I have a message for Comrade Gold," Holten said. "You are invited to a special meeting of the Praesidium."

"Oh!" said Liz, wondering how the Praesidium knew about her.

"We must leave tonight," he said. "We have a long way to go. To Görlitz."

"Where's that?" asked Liz.

"It's to the east, near Poland," replied Comrade Ebert.

Liz felt confused. She was pleased that the Party thought she was important enough to invite to a special meeting, but she was also surprised. She wondered why they were going to travel so far to the east, but she did not feel she could ask any questions.

Holten said, "We can collect your things, and then we can continue the journey immediately."

Liz realized that she had to do what he said. She followed Holten to a black car with a flag on the front. As soon as she and Holten got in, the driver started the engine and drove away.

CHAPTER FOURTEEN
The Tribunal

The **courtroom** was painted white and was about the same size as a school classroom. At one end, guards and members of the Praesidium sat on wooden **benches**. At the other end, Leamas could see the three judges, two men and a woman, sitting at a big table. In front of the table, there were two men sitting on wooden chairs opposite each other. There was a man in a dark suit who was about sixty years old. This must be Karden, thought Leamas. The other man was Fiedler. Leamas sat at the back of the room with a guard on each side of him. He could see Mundt sitting on a bench a few rows in front of him, with policemen all round him.

Suddenly the middle one of the three Tribunal members stood up. She was a small woman in her fifties, with short dark hair. She nodded at a guard to close the door and began to speak. "I am the President of this Tribunal. You all know why we are here. This is a Tribunal that the Praesidium has asked for, and you must remember that what happens here is secret." Then she pointed at Fiedler. "Comrade Fiedler, you can begin."

Fiedler stood up, took some papers from a small bag and began to speak. Leamas thought he talked well – he sounded both serious and confident. "The **case** against Comrade Mundt is that he is an agent working for the British secret service who has given them information," said Fiedler.

"Also, he has received large payments from the British secret service for that information. There is no worse crime than this one, and his sentence has to be a **death sentence**.

"Comrade Mundt is forty-two years old and is Head of Operations for the secret service of the GDR. He was recruited when he was twenty-eight and for many years did special work in Scandinavia – in Norway, Sweden and Finland – so he was able to travel easily to this part of the world. He was good at his job, recruiting agents who worked for us in the West. But he became **greedy** for money, and this is why he has betrayed his country and his people. We have caught him because of his greed for large amounts of money."

Fiedler now looked down at his papers. "At the end of 1956, Mundt was sent to London to work," he said, "but at the end of his time there in the early 1960s, there were problems and two people died. The British wanted to arrest Mundt. Then he disappeared for two days. Surprisingly, after those two days, he took a taxi to a London airport and flew to Berlin. The British police were searching for him, but he was able to leave the country easily because the British secret service had recruited him. I believe that they had told him that they would send him to prison for many years, or he could work as an agent for them.

"If he worked for them, he could return to his country and receive large payments for the information that he gave them."

Fiedler **paused** and looked round the room, then continued.

"We received information some time ago about the large amount of special knowledge that the British secret service had about the GDR. I cannot tell you where that information came from, but it made us believe that someone in our secret service was giving it to them. It had to be someone with an important job, but we were not sure who it was. I wondered if it was Mundt, but it seemed amazing that our own Head of Operations could do this. But then the final evidence was brought to us." He turned to the back of the room. "Bring Leamas forward," he said.

The guards on either side of Leamas stood up and led him forward. They made him stand in front of the table between Fiedler and Karden. The President spoke to him.

"What is your name?" she asked.

"Alec Leamas."

"What is your age?" she continued.

"Fifty."

"What is your job?"

"I work in a library," replied Leamas.

This reply made Fiedler angry. "You worked for the British secret service, didn't you?" he said.

"Yes, that's right," said Leamas.

"You can see from my report," Fiedler went on, speaking to everyone in the room, "that Leamas is a defector from the British secret service. But you will hear suggestions that he is not a defector at all.

"Herr Karden will defend Mundt by saying that Leamas was sent by the British secret service to make us think that Mundt is a traitor. But this is not true. We found Leamas, persuaded him to defect and brought him to the GDR. Leamas was in charge of the East German agents for the British in Berlin, and he does not believe that Mundt is a double agent. But he has given us evidence that helps us to prove that Mundt is a traitor."

Leamas remembered Control's words again: *"Give them your information, and let them work out what to think."* He had done this to Fiedler.

Then Fiedler spoke to Leamas. "The Tribunal has read all the reports of your interrogation," he said. "But I want you to tell them yourself about the operation called Rolling Stone." He turned to the judges. "You have copies of the letters that I will mention," he said.

Fiedler asked Leamas the same questions that he had asked him before, and Leamas talked about the bank accounts in Helsinki and in Copenhagen that he had put money in. Fiedler then explained about the letters that had been sent recently from Leamas to these banks.

"We haven't had a reply from Helsinki," he said. "But we have had a reply from Copenhagen. Leamas deposited ten thousand dollars on 15th June this year, and this money was taken out of the account one week later. Comrade Mundt was in the city for a few days at that time.

"Leamas visited Helsinki on 24th September and deposited forty thousand dollars. Comrade Mundt was in the city for a few days at that time."

There was silence. Then Fiedler continued, "We can also prove that Comrade Mundt arranged the murders of a number of East German double agents so that they did not discover that he was also a British agent. Karl Riemeck was different – he was an agent who worked for Mundt and *knew* that Mundt worked for the British. So Riemeck was a danger to Mundt when I started to suspect that Mundt was a double agent. Mundt told Riemeck to escape because he was in danger, then gave an order to the guards at the checkpoint to shoot him. Later, he killed Riemeck's woman because Riemeck used to talk to her too much about his secret work."

No one spoke. Everyone was looking from Fiedler to Mundt. "This is a greedy, violent man who has betrayed his country and its people," said Fiedler. "For Hans-Dieter Mundt, the only sentence is a death sentence."

CHAPTER FIFTEEN

Confession

The President of the Tribunal turned to the man in the black suit sitting opposite Fiedler. "Comrade Karden," she said, "do you want to talk to the witness, Leamas?"

"Yes, yes, I would like to do that," Karden said, standing up slowly. He put on his glasses, and then he started to speak. "Comrade Mundt believes that Leamas is lying. We know that Karl Riemeck was a traitor, a British spy, but Mundt was not. He did not accept money for betraying our Party. We say that there is no real evidence that he did, but there is evidence that Leamas is part of a British plan. Leamas has involved Comrade Fiedler in this plan to make us think that Comrade Mundt is a traitor."

The man spoke gently and politely. "We say that Leamas pretended to go downhill and to drink too much so that he had to leave his job with the Circus. He pretended to hate his employers. And he hit a shopkeeper so that he was arrested and went to prison. All these things happened to make us think that he was a man who would like to defect and betray his country. He planned to say that Mundt was *not* a traitor, but he gave us evidence that suggested that he *was*. It was a clever plan."

Karden went on in the same polite voice. "We say that the information that Leamas gave to Fiedler, about payments into bank accounts for Mundt, is false.

"The British knew that Fiedler hated Mundt and wanted his job, so they knew that he would help their plan by believing Leamas. But for months, Mundt has known that Fiedler wants to get rid of him, and he has been very careful. It was Mundt who planned our first approach to Leamas in England. And when Leamas was first interrogated, Mundt saw the reports. He saw what Leamas had said about the dates of his visits to banks in Denmark and Finland. Then he was certain that there was a British operation to get rid of him.

"Comrade Mundt then began to check on Leamas's life before his defection. He was looking for a mistake in the plan, and he found one – a very simple one. And he found a witness. But before we talk to the witness, let me ask Mr Leamas a few questions.

"Tell me," said Karden, "do you have much money?"

"Of course not," replied Leamas, angrily. "I wouldn't be here if I had plenty of money."

"Is there someone in England who would lend you money or pay your bills for you?"

"No," said Leamas.

"Thank you," said Karden. "Here's another question. Do you know George Smiley?"

"Yes, of course," replied Leamas. "He was in the Circus. He left it before I did."

"Have you seen him since you left the Circus?" asked Karden.

Leamas paused before he answered because he was not sure why Karden was asking these questions. At last he said, "No."

"And was Smiley interested in you after you left the Circus?" Karden asked.

"No, of course not," replied Leamas.

"And tell me, when you hit the grocer, how much money did you have?"

"Nothing," said Leamas. "I'd been ill for a week and hadn't eaten anything. That's when I decided to defect and–"

Karden interrupted him. "You were owed money by the library, of course, weren't you?"

"How did you know that?" asked Leamas, suddenly worried.

Karden did not answer. "Thank you. You can sit down," he said. Then the guards took Leamas back to his seat on the bench.

The door opened and a large, ugly woman in a grey uniform came in. Behind her was Liz. She came slowly into the courtroom, looking around her. Leamas had forgotten how young she was. When she saw him between the two guards, she stopped.

"Alec!" she said.

One of the guards put his hand on her arm and led her to where Leamas had stood in front of the big table.

"What is your name, child?" asked the President.

"Elizabeth Gold."

"You are a member of the British Communist Party?"

"Yes," replied Liz.

Suddenly there was the noise of furniture falling over on the floor and the sound of Leamas's voice, ugly and loud, shouting, "Leave her alone! Leave her alone!"

Liz turned round and was terrified when she saw a guard hit Leamas hard on his jaw. Two other men got hold of his arms and pulled them behind his back.

Liz saw that his face was white and there was blood on his jaw. Then his head fell forward.

"If he moves again, take him out of the room," said the President. Then she spoke to Liz again. "You know the rule that you must not ask another Comrade for details of what the Party does, don't you?"

Liz nodded. "Yes, of course," she said, quietly.

"Today you must remember that rule. It is better that you don't know any details. We are members of the Party who work for the Praesidium. We are going to ask you some questions, which you must answer. It is important that you speak the truth when you answer them," said the President.

"But who is on trial?" Liz whispered. "Is it Alec?"

"I have told you that it is better you don't know anything. Then you can go home," replied the President. "This man is going to ask you some questions."

The President pointed to Karden, who stood up and spoke politely to Liz.

"Alec Leamas was your lover, wasn't he?" Karden said.

Liz nodded.

"When did you see him last before today?"

"At his flat," she replied. "He was ill. I went to help him."

"I suppose that cost you a lot of money," said Karden. His voice sounded kind, but Liz did not trust him.

"I got the money from Alec," she replied.

"Oh," said Karden, quickly, "so he *did* have money!"

"Oh, God, have I said something wrong?" thought Liz. She was becoming frightened. She wanted to see Leamas's face so she could guess what he wanted her to say. But he was behind her.

"He didn't have much money," she said. "He couldn't pay his bills – they were all paid after he'd gone. A friend paid them."

"Of course," said Karden in his kind voice. "Did you ever meet this friend, Elizabeth?"

She shook her head.

"I see," said Karden.

There was a terrible silence in the courtroom. It was terrifying for Liz because she felt like a blind person in a room full of people who could see. They understood the meaning of her answers, but she did not.

"Do you earn much money, Elizabeth?" asked Karden.

"No," she whispered.

"It must be hard to pay the rent on your flat every month," he said. "Have you paid this month's rent?"

She shook her head again.

"Why not?" asked Karden. "Don't you have any money?"

In a whisper she replied, "Someone bought the **lease** and gave me the flat. They sent it in the post."

"Who?"

"I don't know." Liz was crying now. "Please don't ask any more questions."

But Karden did ask more questions as Liz **sobbed** and sobbed. No one in the courtroom moved. "Tell me," he asked, "did anyone come to see you after Leamas went away?"

"No," she said. She knew that they were trying to hurt Alec, and she did not want to give them any more information.

"But your neighbours have told us that a man came to see you, Elizabeth," he continued. "Who was he?"

"I don't know."

"Who was he?" Karden asked again.

At last, Liz replied. "His name was Smiley. He left his card with his name and address. He said to get in touch with him if I needed any help."

There was complete silence in the court, and then Karden spoke again, pointing towards Leamas. "Leamas had done the one thing the British secret service never expected him to do. He had found a lover – like Riemeck did, in fact. Smiley wanted to know how much Leamas had told the girl."

Then he turned again to Liz and started to ask questions again. "Did you try to get in touch with Leamas?"

"No! He told me not to. He made me promise not to follow him and never to try to find him."

"And the last time you saw him, did you say goodbye?"

Looking very tired, Liz nodded.

"What reason did he give for leaving you?" asked Karden. His voice now sounded ugly.

"He didn't leave me," she said. "He just said there was something he had to do, and afterwards he would come back if he could. He said that things weren't as bad as they seemed . . . and that I would be looked after."

"So that is why you didn't ask about who gave you the lease?"

"Yes." Liz was sobbing again now. "You knew that already, so why did you bring me here?"

Karden waited for her to stop sobbing, then turned to the silent members of the Tribunal. "It is fortunate that Leamas met this girl because now we can be certain that there was an operation against Comrade Mundt. We know that Smiley and the Circus helped the girl."

As Karden quietly sat down, Leamas stood up. The guards did not stop him this time. As he walked to the front of the room, he was trying to work out why the Circus had behaved in this way. "We – Control, Smiley and I – made a careful story to prove that I was a defector," he thought. "But Smiley paid my bills and even bought the lease of Liz's flat and gave it to her. Why would they try to make the operation go wrong? And how do the East Germans know so much about me?"

Leamas couldn't understand it, but he knew that he had to help Liz and Fiedler. He had to make a **confession** about the operation against Mundt.

His face was white as he stood in front of Karden. "Let her go," he said.

Liz was staring at him with tears in her eyes. "No, Alec," she said. "Don't tell them anything because of me."

"It's too late now," said Leamas. Then he turned to the President. "She knows nothing. Send her home. I'll tell you everything."

The President talked quietly to the men on either side of her, then said, "She can leave the court, but she can't go home until the Tribunal has finished."

"She knows nothing!" shouted Leamas. "Karden is right. It was an operation to get rid of Mundt. Let her go."

"She is a witness," replied the woman. "Fiedler may want to question her."

"She knows nothing," said Fiedler. He was sitting with his hands on his knees, looking down at them. "Leamas is right. Let her go." He stood up and led Liz to the door with his arm around her shoulders. Liz looked back at Leamas, but he could not look at her. "Go back to England," said Fiedler, gently, and Liz began to sob as the woman in the grey uniform took her out.

Leamas began to speak to everyone in the room. "Karden is right. After all our East German spies were killed, we – Control,

Smiley and I – decided to get rid of Mundt.

"You know what we did so that you would think I was a defector. Smiley always said the operation could go wrong, but I don't know why he paid my bills and bought the girl's lease."

He turned to the President. "Fiedler hates Mundt, but Mundt isn't an agent for the British. Fiedler just believed in my story. He's a good, honest man, working for his country."

Fiedler smiled and said, "It's strange. The Circus would expect Mundt to check up on Leamas's story, wouldn't they? That's why they made it so good. So I wonder why Smiley paid the bills and bought the lease?"

"I don't know, and I don't know how Mundt found the girl," said Leamas. "I've been very stupid."

"But Mundt hasn't been stupid," said Fiedler, smiling again. "How did he know about the lease? Perhaps he can tell us."

"She increased the amount she paid to the Party every month," Mundt said. "She doesn't earn much money, so I checked why she could suddenly afford to pay more. Then I found out about the lease."

"That's a good answer," replied Fiedler, calmly.

Then the President said, "Comrade Fiedler will not do any more work until the Praesidium has thought about our report. Leamas has already been arrested and Comrade Mundt will decide what to do with him." She looked at Mundt, but he was looking at Fiedler. And as Leamas looked at them both, he suddenly understood the Circus's plan. It was horribly clear.

CHAPTER SIXTEEN
In from the cold

Liz had been in a small, dark room for many hours when she heard footsteps in the corridor outside. She had no idea whether it was day or night. The door opened, and a man stood there without coming into the room. A small amount of blue light from the corridor came into the room so that she recognized him immediately.

"It's Mundt," he said. "Come with me immediately."

Liz was terrified and stood in the middle of the room, not knowing what to do.

"Come on! Hurry!" he said. He stepped into the room, took hold of her arm and led her out into the corridor. She watched, confused, as he locked the door of the room. Then he made her run down a number of badly lit corridors. She noticed that he always checked that no one was coming as they turned into another corridor. Suddenly he stopped, put a key in a door and pushed her outside. She could feel the cold air of the winter evening on her face. He led her forward again, along a path towards a road. Parked by the side of the road was a car. Standing beside it was Alec Leamas.

"Wait here," said Mundt, as he started to move towards Leamas. She waited for a long while as the two men talked quietly to each other. Her body shook because of the cold and her fear. Finally, Mundt returned. "Come with me," he said, and he led her to where Leamas stood.

The two men looked at each other for a moment. "Goodbye," said Mundt. "You're a stupid man, Leamas." And he turned and walked quickly away.

She put out her hand and touched Leamas, but he pushed it away and opened the car door. "Alec," she whispered. "Why is he letting us go?"

"He's letting us go because we've done our job," said Leamas. "Don't think about it. Get in the car."

She got in and asked again, "Why? They said you worked with Fiedler against him."

Leamas did not answer. He started the car and was soon driving along a narrow road. He looked at his watch. "We're five hours away from Berlin," he said. "We need to be there by quarter to one. There's enough time."

For a while, Liz said nothing. Then she said, "You and Mundt are enemies, aren't you?"

Leamas still did not reply. He was driving very fast now, with his tense hands holding the wheel tightly.

"What will happen to Fiedler?" asked Liz, suddenly, and this time Leamas answered.

"Mundt will arrange for him to be shot," he said.

"So why aren't they going to shoot you?" she asked, quickly. "Why has Mundt let you go?"

"All right!" shouted Leamas. "I'll tell you what you and I

weren't supposed to know. Mundt is a double agent. He is a spy for the British secret service. Fiedler worked out that he was a spy, and this is the end of an operation by Control to save Mundt.

"The Circus has used us to kill Fiedler and keep Mundt working for the British. No one will suspect that Mundt is a double agent now."

After a moment, Leamas continued. "Control lied to me. He said that we had to kill Mundt because he was dangerous to the British secret service. He told me that we had to make the East Germans believe Mundt was a double agent. Then they would kill him. I helped to make the plan. It was going to be my last job. I went downhill, lost my job, got the job in the library, hit the grocer, went to prison – you know all that."

"And you became my lover," said Liz.

"That wasn't part of the plan," said Leamas. "My job was to give evidence to Fiedler that Mundt was a spy for the British so that the East Germans would arrest Mundt. I didn't know that Mundt knew everything, including information about you. He sent people to recruit me as a defector and take me to Holland, then Germany. He sent Fiedler to interrogate me. Fiedler believed me and sent his evidence to the Praesidium. But Mundt could prove I wasn't a real defector because he had the information about Smiley and the Circus looking after you, which *they* gave to him. Control didn't tell me about *that* part of the plan."

"But how could the Circus know about me?" Liz cried. "They couldn't make us fall in love!"

"It didn't matter," replied Leamas. "A man called Pitt at the Labour Exchange was working for the Circus. He sent me to the library so I would meet you. The Circus could make it look like we were lovers even if we weren't. And you were a member of the Communist Party, so it was easy to invite you to East Germany. But we made it very easy for them."

"Yes, we did," she said. "We helped them by becoming lovers, and it makes me feel awful. And I still don't understand why he is letting me go. When I get back, I could tell people about this."

"Our escape will help Mundt," replied Leamas. "It will show the Praesidium that there are still double agents in the organization because someone helped us. So they will need Mundt's help to find them."

"So more people can be killed like Fiedler?" asked Liz.

"Fiedler lost, and Mundt won," replied Leamas, shrugging. "That's what happens."

"But Fiedler is a good, honest man," cried Liz. "You said that yourself."

"And Mundt is a horrible, violent man," said Leamas. "But Fiedler is an enemy, on the other side, and Mundt is a friend, on the British side. This is what the secret services are like, Liz. They do bad things so ordinary people like you can sleep safely in their beds."

"It's horrible, Alec!" shouted Liz. "You are as bad as them."

"It's the Cold War, and I hate it, Liz," he replied, sounding very tired. "You've never seen men die like I have."

They were driving along city streets. Leamas was suddenly tense, and he slowed the car. Liz saw a small light moving in front of them. "That's him," Leamas said to himself, quietly. He stopped and opened one of the back doors, and a man got in. Liz did not turn round. She just stared at the rain that was now falling.

"Drive at thirty kilometres an hour. I'll tell you the way," said the man. Liz thought he sounded tense and frightened, and very young. "When we reach the right place, you must get out and run straight to the Wall," he said to Leamas. "The searchlight will shine where you must climb. When the searchlight moves away, begin to climb. The girl must follow you. You'll have to sit on the top and pull the girl up. Do you understand?"

"We understand," replied Leamas. "How long is it before we get there?"

"We will be there in about nine minutes," said the man. "They have only given you a short time. The searchlight will move away at five past one. Then you have ninety seconds to escape. And don't turn back. If you fall or get hurt, keep going. They will shoot anyone they see on this side of the Wall. You must get over it."

"We know," said Leamas.

Leamas drove the car carefully through the dark, wet streets, turning right and left when the young man told him to do so.

"We're nearly there," said the young man.

"Go slowly," he continued. "Now turn left. Turn left!"

They were in a very dark, narrow street. The young man told

Leamas to stop the car and turn off the lights. "Look," he said, pointing down a small street to their left. They could see a small part of the Wall, huge and grey-brown in the yellow lights, with barbed wire on top of it.

"There is a small cut in the wire in the place where you must climb," he said to them. All three of them got out of the car.

"Goodbye," said the young man. Liz looked at his face and knew that he was very frightened.

"Goodbye," she said.

As they were walking along the street, they heard the car drive away. They stopped in the darkness on a small piece of ground not far from the Wall.

"Two minutes to go," said Leamas, looking at his watch. Liz said nothing.

As they watched the searchlight move along the Wall and stop in front of them, Leamas looked at his watch again. "Are you ready?" he asked. Liz nodded.

Leamas took hold of her arm, and they began to walk across the small piece of ground. Liz wanted to run, but he held her arm tightly because he could not really believe that Mundt was letting her go. He did not understand it.

They were almost there when the searchlight moved away and they were in darkness.

Leamas continued walking until he could feel the rough concrete blocks of the Wall with his hand. Looking up, he could just see that there was a small gap in the wire on the top.

There were pieces of metal in the Wall that he could use as steps. Putting his foot on the first one, he started to climb. When he was on the last one, he reached up to pull himself on to the top.

"Come on," he whispered. "Start climbing." He lay down and took hold of her hand as she came to the last metal step. Slowly, he started to pull her up.

Suddenly, enormous lights came on all round them. Leamas was shocked, and it seemed as if he was blind. He still held Liz's hand, but her feet had come off the metal steps, so she was hanging in the air. He called her name and started again to pull her up. Then there was the sound of sirens and shouting. Leamas knelt on the rough concrete and got hold of both of her arms, pulling her to him.

Then they shot her. Leamas felt the shots as they hit her, three or four of them, and her thin arms fell from his hands. He heard a voice shout in English from the other side of the Wall, "Jump, Alec! Jump, man!"

Now there was more shouting. There were English voices and German voices. Leamas heard Smiley's voice, quite close to him. "The girl – where's the girl?"

Leamas put his hand above his eyes to keep the bright lights away and looked down. He saw Liz, lying on the ground. For a moment, he did nothing, and then he began to climb back down the same metal steps. He stood beside her. She was dead.

Nothing happened for a moment, and then they shot him. As he fell next to Liz, Leamas knew that he had finally come in from the cold.

During-reading questions

Write the answers to these questions in your notebook.

CHAPTER ONE

1 Who do you think Alec Leamas works for, and why do you think this?
2 Why is the woman important in this chapter?
3 What goes wrong?

CHAPTER TWO

1 Who is Control, and where does he work?
2 What is the new job that Control discusses with Leamas, and why does he want him to do it?
3 How does Leamas start to prepare for his new job?

CHAPTER THREE

1 Who is Liz, and how does she meet Leamas?
2 How does Liz feel about Leamas, and what worries her?
3 Why do you think that Leamas is ashamed when he leaves Liz's flat?

CHAPTER FOUR

1 How does Ashe make contact with Leamas?
2 "You mustn't involve her in this." Who is Leamas talking about, who is he talking to and why do you think he says this?
3 Leamas says, "How do we know that I was contacted today by the right person?" and Control replies, "We've organized things." Who do you think Control wants Leamas to meet and why?

CHAPTER FIVE

1 Why does Ashe give Leamas an envelope of cash?
2 "His life would never be the same after today." Why do you think Leamas felt like this?

CHAPTER SIX

1 What do you learn about the man who talks to Leamas after Ashe and Kiever?
2 What does Peters tell Leamas that surprises him?
3 Why do you think Leamas thinks about the murdered woman and about Liz?

CHAPTER SEVEN

1 How does Leamas show that he does not believe what Peters believes about an East German agent? How does his behaviour fit with Control's words on pages 40–41?
2 What happens to make Leamas "shocked and confused"?
3 What important decision does Leamas have to make at the end of the chapter?

CHAPTER EIGHT

1 Leamas's landlord describes Leamas's friend as a small man with glasses. Why is this important in the story?
2 Who do you think Smiley is, and why do you think Smiley visits Liz?
3 What opinion do you have of Smiley at the end of the chapter?

CHAPTER NINE

1 Describe Leamas's journey to the farmhouse and what you learn about the farmhouse.

2 What does Leamas pretend to be angry about?

CHAPTER TEN

1 What information do you learn about where the farmhouse is?

2 Control's plan is to make the East German secret service believe Mundt is a traitor. What makes Leamas believe that the plan is working?

CHAPTER ELEVEN

1 How will the letters to the banks help Fiedler to get the information that he wants?

2 What proves to Fiedler that Mundt is a double agent? Why is this important for the story?

3 Think of reasons why Liz has received the invitation to visit the GDR.

CHAPTER TWELVE

1 How does Leamas try to stop himself from being arrested, and why doesn't he succeed?

2 What reasons does Mundt give for putting Leamas and Fiedler on trial?

CHAPTER THIRTEEN

1 How has Fiedler been able to persuade the Praesidium to set up a Tribunal?

2 Why is Liz upset about the number of people who come to the Branch Meeting?

3 What do you think is going to happen next to Liz?

CHAPTER FOURTEEN

1 What does Fiedler say happened when Mundt was in London?

2 What evidence does Fiedler say Leamas has given that shows that Mundt is a traitor?

CHAPTER FIFTEEN

1 What does Karden know about Leamas's job in London that worries Leamas? Why do you think Leamas is worried?

2 How does Liz's information about the lease on her flat and Smiley's visit to her help to show that Leamas is not a real defector?

3 Why does Leamas know he has to make a confession about the operation against Mundt?

CHAPTER SIXTEEN

1 What does the young man do in this chapter?

2 Do you think it was part of Control's plan for Leamas to fall in love with Liz? Give reasons.

3 Leamas does not understand why Mundt has let Liz go. What is the problem with letting her go?

4 Smiley shouts, "The girl – where's the girl?" Give two different reasons why he might have shouted this.

After-reading questions

1 The title of the book is a metaphor. Here is a definition of
a metaphor: *a word or phrase that means one thing and is used
about another thing that is similar.* We could say that someone
"came in from the cold" if they came into a warm house
after they had been for a walk on a cold day. But *The Spy
Who Came in from the Cold* is not about a spy who came home
after a walk. Give your ideas about what the title tells us
about a spy's life. Then say how Leamas has come "in from
the cold" at the end of the story.

2 Look at your answers to "Before-reading questions 4 and 6".
How good were your suggestions?

3 What happens in these places in the story?
   a Berlin
   b Cambridge Circus, London
   c Bywater Street, London
   d Görlitz

4 Who are these characters? What parts do they play in
the story?
   a Ashe
   b Kiever
   c Peters

5 Smiley is on the western side of the Wall when Leamas
and Liz are killed. He sent a short message to Control to
tell him what has happened. Write Smiley's message.

6 Look at your answer to "Before-reading question 5". Was
your explanation of a "secret service" a good one?
Why/Why not?

Exercises

1 Write the correct words in your notebook.

1 piteckcnoh   .....*checkpoint*.......
a place on the line between two countries
where the police check your passport

2 getna   .... another word for a spy

3 nasubocilr   .... You use these to see a very long way. They
are made of two round parts that you
hold against your eyes.

4 scgiarhhtel   .... a large, strong light that is used to look
for people

5 resin   .... a loud noise that is used for warning
people about something

6 tategrnieor   .... to ask someone a lot of questions in a
way that frightens them because you think
they have done something wrong

2 Choose the correct answer. *Example: 1 – c*

1 Where is Leamas flying to?
  a Cambridge
  b Germany
  c London

2 Who says this? "We've got no one left in Germany to protect."
  a Control
  b Leamas
  c Riemeck

3 Who is the East German spy with an unfriendly face?

  a Fiedler

  b Smiley

  c Mundt

4 Why were Leamas's colleagues kind to him at the Circus at first?

  a He borrowed money from them and did not pay it back.

  b They understood that he was having a bad time in his last job.

  c He was angry about the way the Circus had behaved to him.

CHAPTER THREE

3 Rewrite these questions as reported questions in your notebook.

1 "Have you done this kind of work before?" the young woman asked.

The young woman asked if he had done this kind of work before.

2 "Have you got far to go?" Leamas asked Liz.

3 "Alec, what do you believe in?" asked Liz.

4 "Are you religious?" asked Leamas asked Liz.

5 She suddenly cried out, "Alec! Are you leaving?"

6 "Did the grocer push Leamas or not?" the other customers asked each other.

CHAPTER FOUR

4 Read the adjectives. Then write the matching nouns in your notebook. Sometimes the adjective and the noun are the same.

1 rude   ....*rudeness*..........
2 beautiful
3 good
4 boring
5 embarrassed

CHAPTER FIVE

5 Complete these sentences in your notebook, using the names from the box.

Leamas	Ashe	Kiever

1 ....*Leamas*........ did not talk about himself.
2 .... thought Leamas was "one of those cold-war people".
3 .... lived in a small flat in Dolphin Square.
4 .... made a phone call from a public telephone.
5 .... ate at a Chinese restaurant.
6 .... talked about money with Leamas.

6 **Write questions for these answers in your notebook.**

1 Where *did Leamas fly to*?
   He flew to The Hague, in Holland.

2 What ....?
   He was the same height as Leamas but older.

3 Which ....?
   Leamas guessed that Peters came from Russia.

4 How much ....?
   Fifteen thousand pounds now and five thousand for more information during the next year.

5 Who ....?
   Leamas spoke these languages.

6 Why ....?
   Because he listened carefully and only asked a few questions.

7 Why ....?
   Because Peters did not believe that Riemeck could do all the work on his own.

8 Who ....?
   The murdered woman and Liz.

7 **Complete these sentences in your notebook, using the correct form of the words from the box.**

interrogate	withdraw	defect	article
operation	fail	work out	deposit

1 Peters ....*interrogated*.......... Leamas for two days at the house by the sea.

2 Leamas told Peters about a Circus .... called Rolling Stone.

3 Leamas .... thousands of dollars in two different banks.

4 Someone had to use German names in order to .... the money.

5 Control said Leamas had to let the East German agents .... what to think about Leamas's information.

6 The police were searching for Leamas because they thought that he had .... from Britain.

7 There were .... about Leamas in all the English newspapers.

8 Leamas knew that the operation against Mundt would .... if he stopped talking to Peters.

CHAPTER EIGHT

8 **Put the adjectives in the correct group in your notebook.**

confused	special	friendly	strange
	worried	terrified	kind

Example:

Positive meaning	Negative meaning
	confused

CHAPTER NINE

9 **Complete these sentences in your notebook, using the verb forms from the box.**

'll be travelling	wouldn't have	've been travelling
're not going	hadn't found out	've been talking
	would have left	'd known

1 "You*'ll be travelling*........ by car from West Berlin to the East."
2 "I .... all day," thought Leamas.
3 "We .... about what to do with you, since the British discovered your defection."
4 "You .... any further east."
5 "If I .... I was only going to the GDR, I .... defected."
6 "If your colleagues .... about your defection, we .... you in Holland."

CHAPTER TEN

10 **Complete these sentences in your notebook, using the words from the box.**

was going to	would be	used to	ought to
	don't mind	not be easy	

1 When Leamas woke up the next morning, he knew it ....*was going to*....... be a long day.
2 Fiedler was .... interrogating people.
3 That's OK. I .... telling you everything.
4 Leamas knew that Fiedler .... interested in Rolling Stone.
5 It would .... to find out who the payments were for.
6 You .... tell me everything you know.

CHAPTER ELEVEN

11 Complete these sentences in your notebook, using the words from the box.

received	members	trust	managed
expected	organizers	relaxed	tense

1 "I have not ......*received*...... any post from England."
2 He .... to hear from his colleagues in Paris in about a week.
3 Fiedler and Leamas were both .... and Leamas talked a lot about his job.
4 The two men began to like each other and almost to .... each other.
5 It was amazing that Mundt .... to escape.
6 As the days passed he started to seem .... and worried.
7 The letter came from the .... of the Communist Party in Britain.
8 There are going to be visits for .... of your branch to the branch in Leipzig.

CHAPTER TWELVE

12 Order the story by writing *1–9* in your notebook.

a .... Leamas touched the arm of one of the men.
b .... Leamas lay on the floor in pain for hours.
c ....*1*.... Fiedler parked the car at the side of the farmhouse.
d .... Fiedler stood beside Leamas's hospital bed.
e .... Leamas walked in the dark into the guards' bedroom.
f .... Leamas hit the man, and someone hit Leamas.
g .... Suddenly there was shouting, and a door opened violently.
h .... Two people moved forward out of Leamas's bedroom.
i .... Mundt gave Leamas a glass of water.
j .... Leamas kicked a chair into the centre of the room.

13 **Write the opposites of these adjectives in your notebook. There may be more than one word.**

1 quiet ......*noisy, loud*..........

2 awful

3 clever

4 pleased

5 kind

6 upset

14 **Who says these words? Who do they say them to? Write the correct names in your notebook.**

Who spoke?	Who to?

1 "Do you want to talk to the witness, Leamas?"

..*the President*...   ....*Karden*..........

2 "I wouldn't be here if I had plenty of money."

3 "You were owed money by the library, of course, weren't you?"

4 "You are a member of the British Communist Party?"

5 "But who is on trial?"

6 "Oh, so he *did* have money!"

7 "His name was Smiley."

8 "You knew that already, so why did you bring me here?"

9 "Send her home. I'll tell you everything."

10 "Go back to England."

11 "He's a good, honest man, working for his country."

12 "She doesn't earn much money, so I checked why she could suddenly afford to pay more."

CHAPTER SIXTEEN

15 **Correct these sentences in your notebook.**

1 Leamas led Liz out of the building where she had been a prisoner.

Mundt led Liz out of the building where she had been a prisoner.

2 Leamas told Liz that Fiedler was a spy for the British secret service.

3 Control had told Leamas everything about his plan.

4 Fiedler is a horrible, violent man, but he is an enemy of Britain.

5 Leamas and Liz will have nine minutes to escape over the Wall.

6 The young man stopped the car next to the Wall.

7 Leamas and Liz both reached the top of the Wall.

8 Leamas and Liz were shot by the West German border guards.

Project work

1 There was a meeting between Control, Smiley and Peter Guillam (who is an agent who worked for Smiley). It was after they heard that Karl Riemeck was dead and before Leamas came back to the Circus. In this meeting, they made the plan that involves Leamas. Write a play script of this meeting. You must do two things in your play script:

   a Use the story to show your understanding of the plan.

   b Show your ideas about:
   - why they decide not to tell Leamas the whole plan
   - why Smiley does not like the plan.

2 George Smiley is John le Carré's most famous character, and he appears in many of le Carré's novels. Find the meaning of "enigmatic" in a dictionary. Then find all the information about Smiley in this novel, and write your profile of Smiley with these sub-headings:
   - Appearance / age
   - Character
   - Work
   - What he does in this story.

   You can write what you do not know about Smiley as well as what you do know. Then decide: do you agree that Smiley is enigmatic? Why/Why not?

3 We know that Leamas has children. Imagine that Liz also has a child. Those children meet in the 21st century. Both of them know that their father and their mother died at the Berlin Wall, but they do not know any other

details. The Circus did not want anyone to know about what happened. Write a story about the son and daughter finding each other and working together to find the truth about their parents' deaths.

4 Find out about life in East Germany in the 1960s. Write an information booklet or a blog for someone to read before they read *The Spy Who Came in from the Cold*. You can find lots of interesting information on the internet, but remember to write your booklet or blog in your own words. Include photos, illustrations or maps.

An answer key for all questions and exercises can be found at **www.penguinreaders.co.uk**

Essay questions

1 Explain what you have learned about what the secret services did during the Cold War. Then explain what you have learned about the people in the story who worked for the secret services. Compare what they believed and how they felt. Use quotations from these sections of the story to help you. (500 words)

Chapter Two, Control – pages 13–14

- "In our jobs, we don't care about each other, do we? But we aren't like that really, are we? I mean . . . we can't be out in the cold all the time."

- "In our work, we do bad things so that ordinary people can sleep safely in their beds . . ."

- "And since the war, our methods have become quite similar to the methods of the other side."

- "But of course, *we* use these methods for the right reasons. We have to be as ruthless as them, even though our government's reasons are better than theirs."

page 16

- "After all, we all get burned out in the end, in this job. We don't hate or love anyone or anything – but we don't want there to be any more pain."

Chapter Ten, Fiedler and Leamas – pages 51–52

- Most of all, he wanted to know about why they worked for the Circus. "What do they believe in? What is their philosophy?" he asked.

"I don't know," said Leamas. "They don't believe in anything. They're just people."

"What makes them do these jobs, then?" asked Fiedler. He sounded confused.

"I don't know," said Leamas. Then he added, "I suppose they don't like Communists."

"I see," said Fiedler. "We kill people because we believe in something. It must be harder to kill people if you don't have a philosophy that you believe in."

"I don't know," replied Leamas. "And I don't care."

Chapter Sixteen – page 82

• "And Mundt is a horrible, violent man," said Leamas. "But Fiedler is an enemy, on the other side, and Mundt is a friend, on the British side. This is what the secret services are like, Liz. They do bad things so ordinary people like you can sleep safely in their beds."

"It's horrible, Alec!" shouted Liz. "You are as bad as them."

"It's the Cold War and I hate it, Liz," he replied, sounding very tired.

2 Explain the differences between Communism in Eastern Europe and democracy in the West after World War II. Then explain why you think Liz might be a Communist and why Leamas laughed when she told him that she was a Communist. (500 words)

Glossary

agent (n.)
another word for a *spy*

a number of (phr.)
a number of things or people
means a few of them or
several of them

article (n.)
a story in a newspaper or
magazine

ashamed (adj.)
You feel *ashamed* when you feel
guilty because you have done
something wrong.

beat (someone) up (phr. v.)
to attack and hurt someone using
your hands and feet

bench (n.)
a long, hard seat for two or more
people. They are usually in
courtrooms or outside.

betray (v.)
If you *betray* a person, you break
a promise you made to them or
you tell other people their secret.

binoculars (n.)
You use *binoculars* to see a very
long way. They are made of
two round parts that you hold
against your eyes.

bitterly (adv.)
You talk about an experience
bitterly when you feel angry about
it. If the weather is *bitterly* cold, it
is extremely cold.

bloody (adj.)
People use *bloody* before a word
when they are angry about it.
This is a rude word.

branch (n.)
all the members of a group in a
certain area

burned out (adj.)
very tired from working too hard

career (n.)
the most important job or jobs
that you do through your life

put a case (phr. v.); **case** (n.)
A *case* is a matter that is decided
by a judge. You *put a case* against
someone when you give reasons
why they should go to prison.

cash (n.)
money, as paper or coins

checkpoint (n.)
a place on the line between two
countries where the police check
your passport

chequebook (n.)
a book that contains cheques
(= small pieces of paper from
your bank that you sign and use
to pay for things)

colleague (n.)
a person who you work with

comrade (n.)
a word used for talking about
members of the Communist
Party by other members of the
Communist Party

confession (n.)
You make a *confession* when
you admit that you have done
something wrong.

courtroom (n.)
a place where a judge decides
if someone will go to prison for
a crime

cross (adj.)
angry

current statement (n.)
information from your bank
that tells you how much money
you have in your account

defector (n.); **defect** (v.);
defection (n.)
When someone *defects*, they
leave one group of people and
go to another one. This act is
called *defection*. A person who
does this is a *defector*.

deposit (v.)
You *deposit* money when you pay
it into a bank account.

details (n.)
information about you, like
your name, address and
telephone number

double agent (n.)
someone who is a spy for a
government but who also helps
that *government's* enemy

embarrassed (adj.)
feeling worried about what
people will think of you because
of something you have done or
forgotten to do

encyclopaedia (n.)
a large book that contains
information about many
different subjects

evidence (n.)
something that helps to prove
that a person is guilty of a crime

farmhouse (n.)
the main house on a farm, where the farmer lives

get in touch (phr. v.)
to contact someone

get rid of (phr. v.)
to make something go away because you do not want it with you any more

go downhill (phr. v.)
If someone *goes downhill*, they stop taking care of themselves and they stop succeeding in their life or in their job.

government (n.)
a group of important people who decide what must happen in a country

greedy (adj.)
A *greedy* person wants more and more of something, like food or money.

grocer's shop (n.); **groceries** (n.)
a small shop where you can buy food and things for the home. These things are called *groceries*.

guard (n.)
a soldier whose job is to watch and protect a place. *Guards* check that people have the correct documents when they cross from one country to another.

Head of Operations (pr. n.)
the person who is responsible for all the activities in a company

in charge (phr.);
in charge of (phr.)
If you are *in charge*, you are responsible for people in a group. If you are *in charge of* people, you are responsible for them.

interrogate (v.);
interrogation (n.)
to ask someone a lot of questions because you think they have done something wrong. This situation is called an *interrogation*.

involve (v.)
If you *involve* someone in a situation, you include them in it so that they are affected by it.

Iron Curtain (pr. n.)
the name for the line between Eastern Europe and the rest of Europe between 1947 and 1991. *Iron* is a hard, heavy metal. A *curtain* is a long piece of material that hangs down between two areas.

I suppose so (phr.)
You say *I suppose so* when you agree with someone but you are not completely sure about it.

jaw (n.)
Your *jaws* are the bones in your face that hold your teeth.

knowledge (n.)
the things that you know

Labour Exchange (pr. n.)
in the past, an office where you could go to find a job

landlord (n.)
the man who owns the house or flat that you live in. If a woman owns it, she is a *landlady*.

lean (v.)
If you *lean* something against a wall, you put it against the wall to stop it falling.

lease (n.)
a document showing that you are allowed to live in or use a certain building

luggage (n.)
the bags and cases that you take with you when you travel

method (n.)
a way of doing something

Official Secrets Act (pr. n.)
in the UK, a law that stops people from knowing what is in some *government* documents

operation (n.)
1. When a *spy* works on an *operation*, they take part in a planned activity.
2. When someone is ill, they could need an *operation*.

other side (n.)
people who work for the enemy

pause (n. and v.)
If you *pause*, you stop speaking or moving for a few seconds and then start again.

payment (n.)
an amount of money that someone gives you for doing a job

Praesidium (pr. n.)
in the Soviet Union, a special group of important people who worked for the Communist Party

pretend (v.)
to make people think that something is true when it is not

recruit (v.)
to give someone a job

run out (phr. v.)
When your passport *runs out*, you cannot use it any more after a certain date, and you must ask for a new one.

ruthless (adj.)
A *ruthless* person does not worry about causing pain to other people.

searchlight (n.)
a large, strong light that is used to look for people

sentence (v. and n.); **death sentence** (n.)
A *sentence* is the time that someone must stay in prison. When someone is *sentenced*, the judge tells them how much time they must stay in prison. If someone is given a *death sentence*, they will be punished by death.

shave (v.)
When a man *shaves*, he cuts his beard off his face.

shrug (v.)
to move your shoulders up and then down to show that you do not know something or that you do not care very much

siren (n.)
a loud noise that is used for warning people about something

sob (v.)
to cry loudly

Soviet (pr. n.)
connected with the large area that belonged to Russia between 1947 and 1991

Special Branch (pr. n.)
in the UK, the special group of police who try to solve crimes against the *government*

spy (v. and n.)
someone whose job is to find out secrets from their country's enemies. Someone who *spies* has this job.

suggestion (n.); **suggest** (v.)
If you *suggest* something, you offer an idea for people to consider. When you do this, you make a *suggestion*.

suspect (v.)
to strongly believe something about someone

sweat (v.)
to produce small drops of water through your skin because you are hot or ill

tense (adj.)
nervous; not relaxed

terrified (adj.)
very frightened

trial (n.); **to be put on trial**
(phr. v.)
when a judge listens to all the
evidence for and against a person
and decides if they are guilty or
not. People are *put on trial* if they
are *suspected* of a crime.

withdraw (v.)
If you *withdraw* money, you take
it out of a bank account.

witness (n.)
a person who sees a crime

work out (phr. v.)
to understand something after
considering all the information
and *evidence*

Penguin Readers

Visit **www.penguinreaders.co.uk**
for FREE Penguin Readers resources
and digital and audio versions of this book.